Compulsory Mis-Education

BOOKS BY PAUL GOODMAN

*The Community of Scholars*
*Growing Up Absurd*
*Utopian Essays and Practical Proposals*
*Drawing the Line*
*Communitas* (with Percival Goodman)
*Gestalt Therapy* (with F. S. Perls and Ralph Hefferline)
*Art and Social Nature*
*Kafka's Prayer*
*The Structure of Literature*
*The Society I Live In Is Mine*
*Compulsory Mis-Education*

*The Lordly Hudson and Other Poems*
*The Empire City*
*The Break-Up of Our Camp*
*Parents' Day*
*Stop-Light and Other Noh Plays*
*The Facts of Life*
*Making Do*
*Our Visit to Niagara*

# Compulsory Mis- -education

# Paul Goodman

HORIZON PRESS

New York

*For Mabel*

"One had to cram all this stuff into one's mind, whether one liked it or not. This coercion had such a deterring effect that, after I had passed the final examination, I found the consideration of any scientific problems distasteful to me for an entire year. . . . It is in fact nothing short of a miracle that the modern methods of instruction have not yet entirely strangled the holy curiosity of inquiry; for this delicate little plant, aside from stimulation, stands mainly in need of freedom; without this it goes to wrack and ruin without fail. It is a very grave mistake to think that the enjoyment of seeing and searching can be promoted by means of coercion and a sense of duty. To the contrary, I believe that it would be possible to rob even a healthy beast of prey of its voraciousness, if it were possible, with the aid of a whip, to force the beast to devour continuously, even when not hungry—especially if the food, handed out under such coercion, were to be selected accordingly."

—Albert Einstein
(quoted in *Examining in Harvard College*)

# Contents

PART THREE    College

# Preface

## I

In these remarks on the schools, I do not try to be generous or fair, but I have seen what I am talking about and I hope I am rational. The case is that we have been swept and are being swept on a flood-tide of public policy and popular sentiment into an expansion of schooling and an aggrandizement of school-people that is grossly wasteful of wealth and effort and does positive damage to the young. Yet I do not hear any fundamental opposition in principle, nor even prudent people (rather than stingy people) saying, go warily. The dominance of the present school auspices prevents any new thinking about education, although we face unprecedented conditions.

It is uncanny. When, at a meeting, I offer that perhaps we already have too much formal schooling and that, under present conditions, the more we get the less education we will get, the others look at me oddly and proceed to discuss how to get more money for schools and how to upgrade the schools. I realize suddenly that I am confronting a mass superstition.

In this little book, I keep resorting to the metaphor school-monks: the administrators, professors, academic sociologists, and licensees with diplomas who have proliferated into an invested intellectual class worse than anything since the time of Henry the Eighth. Yet I am convinced—as they get their grants and buildings and State laws that give them sole competence—that the monks are sincere in their bland faith in the school. The schools provide the best preparation for everybody for a complicated world, are the logical haven for unemployed youth, can equalize opportunity for the underprivileged, administer research in all fields, and be the indispensable mentor for creativity, business-practice, social work, mental hygiene, genuine literacy—name it, and there are credits for it leading to a degree. The schools offer very little evidence of their unique ability to perform any of these things—there is plenty of evidence to the contrary—but they do not need to offer evidence, since nobody opposes them or proposes alternatives.

A major pressing problem of our society is the defective structure of the economy that advantages the upper middle-class and excludes the lower class. The school-people and Ph.D. sociologists loyally take over also this problem, in the war on poverty, the war against delinquency, retraining those made jobless, training the Peace Corps, and so forth. But as it turns out, just by taking over the problem, they themselves gobble up the budgets and confirm the defective structure of the economy.

And inevitably, expanding and aggrandizing, becoming the universal trainer, baby-sitter, and fix-it, the schools are losing the beautiful academic and community functions that by nature they do have.

## II

The ideas in this book were called up for specific busy occasions. The remarks on the drop-outs were the substance of a contribution to a national conference on the problem, called by the National Education Association. The notes on psychosomatic education were, first, the report of a school visit when I was a member of a local school board in New York; the note on progressive education was a recruiting talk for a Summerhill-variant school of which I am a trustee. The remarks on the Secretary of Labor's proposal and on the hang-ups of getting a job were asked for by the National Committee on Employment of Youth, and printed in *The American Child*. The discussion of adolescent difficulties in com-

munication was commissioned for a freshman course at
the University of Western Michigan; and the discussion
of unteachability was commissioned by the Methodists
for a freshman-orientation program. The critique of programmed instruction was part of a controversy in the
*Harvard Educational Review*. The analysis of teaching
science was the gist (as I saw it) of a couple of seminars
with people from the government science institutes that I
attended at the Institute for Policy Studies in Washington. And the proposals for the liberal arts colleges were
the gist of a section at the 1964 meeting of the Association
for Higher Education.

(At that meeting, I asked the A.H.E. to urge
society to find various other means of coping with
youth unemployment, rather than putting the entire burden on the colleges. Not surprisingly, this modest resolution went crashingly nowhere.)

Re-writing, I have kept in evidence these busy and
polemical contexts. For this where my story is. John
Dewey somewhere makes the remarkable observation
that the essential part of philosophy is the philosophy of
education, the rest being the subject of special sciences.
But I am not able, or prepared, to write such a philosophy. What I can, and do, write is this fighting recall to
plain sense, holding action, attempt to lay the ground-
work of a decent future.

## III

The immediate future of our country seems to me to have two looming prospects, both gloomy. If the powers-that-be proceed as stupidly, timidly, and "politically" as they have been doing, there will be a bad breakdown and the upsurge of a know-nothing fascism of the right. Incidentally, let me say that I am profoundly unimpressed by our so-called educational system when, as has happened, Governor Wallace comes from the South as a candidate in Northern states and receives his highest number of votes (in some places a majority) in suburbs that have had the *most* years of schooling, more than 16.

The other prospect—which, to be frank, seems to me to be the goal of the school-monks themselves—is a progressive regimentation and brainwashing, on scientific principles, directly toward a fascism-of-the-center, 1984. Certainly this is not anybody's deliberate purpose; but given the maturing of automation, and the present dominance of the automating spirit in schooling, so that all of life becomes geared to the automatic system, that is where we will land.

Therefore in this book I do not choose to be "generous" and "fair."

## IV

Underlying the present superstitution, however, is an objective fact. Major conditions of modern life *are* unprecedented and we do not know how to cope with them. Confused, people inevitably try to ward off anxiety by rigidifying the old methods of dominant economic and intellectual groups. Omitting the changed international conditions, let me just mention some unprecedented domestic developments that are crucial for even primary education.

Within the United States, we have reached a point of productivity when it becomes absurd to use the rate of growth and the Gross National Product as measures of economic health. To be useful, new production must be much more narrowly qualified, e.g. serve the public sector or eliminate grinding poverty. Unqualified growth already does more harm than good. Thus, we must consider concepts like "work" and "leisure" and "unemployment" in a new way, and we must begin to distinguish between economic well-being and mere affluence. Yet only a handful of economists are thinking along these lines, and almost no one escapes the mesmerism of the GNP. We cannot expect educators to be far ahead.

Correspondingly, the social valuation of scientific technology and science must change. Up to now, the emphasis has been on the products, including the research products, the Knowledge Explosion. But these become diminishingly useful, and the more they flood the environment, the less skillful the average man becomes. The problem for general education, rather, is to learn to *live* in a high technology. The emphasis ought to be on the moral virtues of science itself, both austere and liberating; on its humane beauty; on the selectivity and circumspect reasonableness of sciences like ecology and psychosomatic medicine. These are very different values from the present gearing of general education to the processing of Ph.D.'s.

Urbanization is almost total; independent farming, farming as "a way of life," is at the point of extinction. Yet this development is unexamined and uncontrolled. The disastrous pattern of blighted center, suburbs, and conurbation is taken for granted, and highway, tax, housing, and schooling policies serve only to intensify it. Then astoundingly, we come to suffer from what looks like a population explosion, even though, in this country, vast and beautiful regions are being depopulated. One weeps to see it, yet nothing is done to find possible principles of rural recovery and better balance. Or, in the dense cities, to find functional equivalents for the lost self-reliance, extended family, and community.

There is anomie and an alarming rate of urban mental illness. My own view is that an important factor in these is powerlessness; it is impossible to become engaged or usefully to identify when one cannot initiate and have a say in deciding. If this is so, we should be studying new patterns of decentralizing while we centralize. But there are no such studies and, in my opinion, the bureaucratic methods of social psychiatry probably worsen the social diseases. Certainly we are in a political crisis, for, though the forms of democracy are intact, the content is vanishing. Such political vitality as there is finds its expression in paralegal ways; but these will eventually either renovate the constitution or degenerate into violence and gross injustice. Meantime, there is a proliferation of media of communication and messages communicated, for people need to be informed and want to be informed; yet, partly just because of the communications, there is brainwashing and conformity.

Such are some of the extraordinary conditions for which our schooling fails to educate. It is essential to find alternative ways of educating.

North Stratford, New Hampshire
July 1964

# Part one

# *Primary Grades*

# 1

# The universal

# trap

I

A conference of experts on school drop-outs will discuss the background of poverty, cultural deprivation, race prejudice, family and emotional troubles, neighborhood uprooting, urban mobility. It will explore ingenious expedients to counteract these conditions, though it will not much look to remedying them—that is not its business. And it will suggest propaganda—e.g. no school, no job— to get the youngsters back in school. It is axiomatic that they ought to be in school.

After a year, it proves necessary to call another conference to cope with the alarming fact that more than 75% of the drop-outs who have been cajoled into returning, have dropped out again. They persist in failing; they still are not sufficiently motivated. What curricular changes must there be? how can the teachers learn the life-style of the underprivileged?

Curiously muffled in these conferences is the question that puts the burden of proof the other way: What are they drop-outs from? Is the schooling really good for them, or much good for anybody? Since, for many, there are such difficulties with the present arrangements, might not some better arrangements be invented? Or bluntly, since schooling undertakes to be compulsory, must it not continually review its claim to be useful? Is it the only means of education? Isn't it unlikely that *any* single type of social institution could fit almost every youngster up to age 16 and beyond? (It is predicted that by 1970, 50% will go to college.)

But conferences on drop-outs are summoned by school professionals, so perhaps we cannot hope that such elementary questions will be raised. Yet neither are they raised by laymen. There is a mass superstition, underwritten by additional billions every year, that adolescents must continue going to school. The middle-class *know* that no professional competence—i.e. status and salary—can be attained without many diplomas; and poor people have allowed themselves to be convinced that the primary remedy for their increasing deprivation is to agitate for better schooling. Nevertheless, I doubt that, *at present or with any reforms that are conceivable under present school administration,* going to school is the best use for the time of life of the majority of youth.

## II

Education is a natural community function and occurs inevitably, since the young grow up on the old, toward their activities, and into (or against) their institutions; and the old foster, teach, train, exploit, and abuse the young. Even neglect of the young, except physical neglect, has an educational effect—not the worst possible.

Formal schooling is a reasonable auxiliary of the inevitable process, whenever an activity is best learned by singling it out for special attention with a special person to teach it. Yet it by no means follows that the complicated artifact of a school system has much to do with education, and certainly not with good education.

Let us bear in mind the way in which a big school system might have nothing to do with education at all. The New York system turns over $700 millions annually, not including capital improvements. There are 750 schools, with perhaps 15 annually being replaced at an extra cost of $2 to $5 millions each. There are 40,000 paid employees. This is a vast vested interest, and it is very probable that—like much of our economy and almost all of our political structure, of which the public schools are a part—it goes on for its own sake, keeping more than a million people busy, wasting wealth, and pre-empting time and space in which something else could be going on. It is a gigantic market for textbook manufacturers, building contractors, and graduate-schools of Education.

The fundamental design of such a system is ancient, yet it has not been altered although the present operation is altogether different in scale from what it was, and therefore it must have a different meaning. For example, in 1900, 6% of the 17-year-olds graduated from high school, and less than ½% went to college; whereas in 1963, 65% graduated from high school and 35% went on to something called college. Likewise, there is a vast difference between schooling intermitted in life on a farm or in a city with plenty of small jobs, and schooling that is a child's only "serious" occupation and often his only adult contact. Thus, a perhaps outmoded institution has become almost the only allowable way of growing up. And with this pre-empting, there is an increasing intensification of the one narrow experience, e.g. in the shaping of the curriculum and testing according to the increasing requirements of graduate schools far off in time and place. Just as our American society as a whole is more and more tightly organized, so its school system is more and more regimented as part of that organization.

In the organizational plan, the schools play a non-educational and an educational role. The non-educational role is very important. In the tender grades, the schools are a baby-sitting service during a period of collapse of the old-type family and during a time of extreme urbanization and urban mobility. In the junior and senior high school grades, they are an arm of the police, providing cops and concentration camps paid for in the budget under the heading "Board of Education." The educational role is, by and large, to provide—at public and parents' expense—apprentice-training for corporations, government, and the teaching profession itself, and also to train the young, as New York's Commissioner of Education has said (in the Worley case), "to handle constructively their problems of adjustment to authority."

The public schools of America have indeed been a powerful, and beneficent, force for the democratizing of a great mixed population. But we must be careful to keep reassessing them when, with changing conditions, they become a universal trap and democracy begins to look like regimentation.

## III

Let me spend a page on the history of the compulsory nature of the school systems. In 1961, in *The Child, the Parent, and the State,* James Conant mentions a possible incompatibility between "individual development" and "national needs"; this, to my mind, is a watershed in American philosophy of education and puts us back to the ideology of Imperial Germany, or on a par with contemporary Russia.

When Jefferson and Madison conceived of compulsory schooling, such an incompatibility would have been unthinkable. They were in the climate of the Enlightenment, were strongly influenced by Congregational (town-meeting) ideas, and were of course makers of a revolution. To them, "citizen" meant society-*maker*, not one "participating in" or "adjusted to" society. It is clear that they regarded themselves and their friends as citizens existentially, so to speak; to make society was their breath of life. But obviously such conceptions are worlds removed from, and diametrically opposed to, our present political reality, where the ground rules and often the score are pre-determined.

For Jefferson, people had to be taught in order to multiply the sources of citizenly initiative and to be vigilant for freedom. Everybody had to become literate and study history, in order to make constitutional innovations and be fired to defend free institutions, which was presumably the moral that history taught. And those of good parts were to study a technological natural philosophy, in order to make inventions and produce useful goods for the new country. By contrast, what are the citizenly reasons for which we compel everybody to be literate, etc.? To keep the economy expanding, to understand the mass-communications, to choose between indistinguishable Democrats and Republicans. Planning and decision-making are lodged in top managers; rarely, and at most, the electorate serves as a pressure-group. There is a new emphasis on teaching science—we will discuss this in another context—but the vast majority will never use this knowledge and will forget it; they are consumers.

Another great impulse for compulsory education came from the new industrialism and urbanism during the three or four decades after the Civil War, a time

also of maximum immigration. Here the curricular demands were more mundane: in the grades, literacy and
arithmetic; in the colleges, professional skills to man
the expanding economy. But again, no one would have
spoken of an incompatibility between 'individual development" and "national needs," for it was considered to
be an open society, abounding in opportunity. Typically,
the novels of Horatio Alger, Jr., treat schooling as
morally excellent as well as essential for getting ahead;
and there is no doubt that the immigrants saw education-
for-success as also a human value for their children.
Further, the school-system was not a trap. The 94%
who in 1900 did not finish high school had other life
opportunities, including making a lot of money and
rising in politics. But again, by and large this is not our
present situation. There is plenty of social mobility,
opportunity to rise—except precisely for the ethnic
minorities who are our main concern as drop-outs—but
the statuses and channels are increasingly stratified,
rigidified, cut and dried. Most enterprise is parceled out
by feudal corporations, or by the state; and these determine the requirements. Ambition with average talent
meets these rules or fails; those without relevant talent,
or with unfortunate backgrounds, cannot even survive
in decent poverty. The requirements of survival are
importantly academic, attainable only in schools and
universities; but such schooling is ceasing to have an
initiating or moral meaning.

We do not have an open economy; even when jobs
are not scarce, the corporations and state dictate the

possibilities of enterprise. General Electric swoops down on the high schools, or IBM on the colleges, and skims off the youth who have been pre-trained for them at public or private expense. (Private college tuition runs upward of $6000, and this is estimated as a third or less of the actual cost for "education and educational administration.") Even a department store requires a diploma for its salespeople, not so much because of the skills they have learned as that it guarantees the right character: punctual and with a smooth record. And more generally, since our powers-that-be have opted for an expanding economy with a galloping standard of living, and since the powers of the world are in an arms and space race, there *is* a national need for many graduates specifically trained. Thus, even for those selected, the purpose is irrelevant to citizenly initiative, the progress of an open society, or personal happiness, and the others have spent time and effort in order to be progressively weeded out. Some drop out.

## IV

It is said that our schools are geared to "middle-class values," but this is a false and misleading use of terms. The schools less and less represent *any* human values, but simply adjustment to a mechanical system.

Because of the increasing failure of the schools with

the poor urban mass, there has developed a line of criticism—e.g. Oscar Lewis, Patricia Sexton, Frank Riessman, and even Edgar Friedenberg—asserting that there is a "culture of poverty" which the "middle-class" schools do not fit, but which has its own virtues of spontaneity, sociality, animality. The implication is that the "middle class," for all its virtues, is obsessional, prejudiced, prudish.

Pedagogically, this insight is indispensable. A teacher must try to reach each child in terms of what he brings, his background, his habits, the language he understands. But if taken to be more than technical, it is a disastrous conception. The philosophic aim of education must be to get each one out of his isolated class and into the one humanity. Prudence and responsibility are not middle class virtues but human virtues; and spontaneity and sexuality are not powers of the simple but of human health. One has the impression that our social-psychologists are looking not to a human community but to a future in which the obsessionals will take care of the impulsives!

In fact, some of the most important strengths that have historically belonged to the middle class are flouted by the schools: independence, initiative, scrupulous honesty, earnestness, utility, respect for thorough scholarship. Rather than bourgeois, our schools have become petty-bourgeois, bureaucratic, time-serving, gradgrind-practical, timid, and *nouveau riche* climbing. In the upper grades and colleges, they often exude a cynicism that belongs to rotten aristocrats.

Naturally, however, the youth of the poor and of the middle class respond differently to the petty bourgeois atmosphere. For many poor children, school is orderly and has food, compared to chaotic and hungry homes, and it might even be interesting compared to total deprivation of toys and books. Besides, the wish to improve a child's lot, which on the part of a middle class parent might be frantic status-seeking and pressuring, on the part of a poor parent is a loving aspiration. There is here a gloomy irony. The school that for a poor Negro child might be a great joy and opportunity is likely to be dreadful; whereas the middle class child might be better off *not* in the "good" suburban school he has.

Other poor youth, herded into a situation that does not fit their disposition, for which they are unprepared by their background, and which does not interest them, simply develop a reactive stupidity very different from their behavior on the street or ball field. They fall behind, play truant, and as soon as possible drop out. If the school situation is immediately useless and damaging to them, their response must be said to be life-preservative. They thereby somewhat diminish their chances of a decent living, but we shall see that the usual propaganda—that schooling is a road to high salaries—is for most poor youth a lie; and the increase in security is arguably not worth the torture involved.

The reasonable social policy would be not to have these youth in school, certainly not in high school, but to educate them otherwise and provide opportunity for a decent future in some other way. How? I shall venture some suggestions later; in my opinion, the wise thing would be to have our conferences on *this* issue, and omit the idea of drop-out altogether. But the brute fact is that our society isn't really interested; the concern for the drop-outs is mainly because they are a nuisance and a threat and can't be socialized by the existing machinery.

Numerically far more important than these overt drop-outs at 16, however, are the children who conform to schooling between the ages of 6 to 16 or 20, but who drop out internally and day-dream, their days wasted, their liberty caged and scheduled. And there are many such in the middle class, from backgrounds with plenty of food and some books and art, where the youth is seduced by the prospect of money and status, but even more where he is terrified to jeopardize the only pattern of life he knows.

It is in the schools and from the mass media, rather than at home or from their friends, that the mass of our citizens in all classes learn that life is inevitably routine, depersonalized, venally graded; that it is best to toe the mark and shut up; that there is no place for spontaneity, open sexuality, free spirit. Trained in the schools, they go on to the same quality of jobs, culture, politics. This *is* education, mis-education, socializing to the national norms and regimenting to the national "needs."

John Dewey used to hope, naively, that the schools could be a community somewhat better than society and serve as a lever for social change. In fact, our schools reflect our society closely, except that they *emphasize* many of its worst features, as well as having the characteristic defects of academic institutions of all times and places.


# V


Let us examine realistically half a dozen aspects of the school that is dropped out *from*.

(a) There is widespread anxiety about the children not learning to read, and hot and defensive argument about the methods of teaching reading. Indeed, reading deficiency is an accumulating scholastic disadvantage that results in painful feeling of inferiority, truancy, and drop-out. Reading is crucial for school success—all subjects depend on it—and therefore for the status-success that the diploma is about. Yet in all the anxiety and argument, there is no longer any mention of the freedom and human cultivation that literacy is supposed to stand for.

In my opinion, there is something phony here. For a change, let us look at this "reading" coldly and ask if it is really such a big deal except precisely in the school that is supposed to teach it and is sometimes failing to do so.

With the movies, TV, and radio that the illiterate also share, there is certainly no lack of "communications."

We cannot say that as humanities or science, the reading-matter of the great majority is in any way superior to the content of these other media. And in the present stage of technology and economy, it is probably *less* true than it was in the late nineteenth century—the time of the great push to universal literacy and arithmetic—that the mass-teaching of reading is indispensable to operate the production and clerical system. It is rather our kind of urbanism, politics, and buying and selling that require literacy. These are not excellent.

Perhaps in the present dispensation we should be as well off if it were socially acceptable for large numbers not to read. It would be harder to regiment people if they were not so well "informed"; as Norbert Wiener used to point out, every repetition of a cliché only increases the noise and *prevents* communication. With less literacy, there would be more folk culture. Much suffering of inferiority would be avoided if young-sters did not have to meet a perhaps unnecessary standard. Serious letters could only benefit if society were less swamped by trash, lies, and bland verbiage. Most im-portant of all, *more* people might become genuinely literate if it were understood that reading is not a matter-of-course but a *special useful art with a proper subject-matter, imagination and truth*, rather than a means of communicating top-down decisions and advertising. (The advertising is a typical instance: when the purpose of advertising was to give information—"New shipment of salt fish arrived, very good, foot of Barclay Street"—it was useful to be able to read; when the point of advertising is to create a synthetic demand, it is better not to be able to read.)

(b) Given their present motives, the schools are not competent to teach authentic literacy, reading as a means of liberation and cultivation. And I doubt that most of us who seriously read and write the English language ever learned it by the route of "Run, Spot, Run" to *Silas Marner*. Rather, having picked up the rudiments either in cultured homes or in the first two grades, we really learned to read by our own will and free exploration, following our bent, generally among books that are considered inappropriate by school librarians!

A great neurologist tells me that the puzzle is not how to teach reading, but why some children fail to learn to read. Given the amount of exposure that any urban child gets, any normal human animal should spontaneously catch on to the code. What prevents? It is almost demonstrable that, for many children, it is precisely going to school that prevents—because of the school's alien style, banning of spontaneous interest, extrinsic rewards and punishments. (In many under-privileged schools, the I.Q. steadily falls the longer they go to school.) Many of the backward readers might have had a better chance on the streets.

But let me say something, too, about the "successful" teaching of reading and writing in the schools. Consider, by contrast, the method employed by Sylvia Ashton-Warner in teaching little Maoris. She gets them to ask for their *own* words, the particular gut-word of fear, lust, or despair that is obsessing the child that day; this is written for him on strong cardboard; he learns it instantaneously and never forgets it; and soon he has an exciting, if odd, vocabulary. From the beginning, writing is by demand, practical, magical; and of course it is simply an extension of speech—it is the best and strongest speech, as writing should be. What is read is what somebody is importantly trying to tell. Now what do our schools do? We use tricks of mechanical conditioning. These do positive damage to spontaneous speech, meant expression, earnest understanding. Inevitably, they create *in the majority* the wooden attitude toward "writing," as entirely different from speech, that college-teachers later try to cope with in Freshman Composition. And reading inevitably becomes a manipulation of signs, e.g. for test-passing, that has no relation to experience.

(Until recently, the same discouragement by school-teachers plagued children's musical and plastic expression, but there have been attempts to get back to spontaneity—largely, I think, because of the general revolution in modern art and musical theory. In teaching science, there is just now a strong movement to encourage imagination rather than conditioned "answers." In teaching foreign languages, the emphasis is now strongly on vital engagement and need to speak. Yet in teaching reading and writing, the direction has been the contrary; even progressive education has gone back to teaching spelling. These arts are regarded merely as "tools.")

(c) The young rightly resist animal constraint. But,

at least in New York where I have been a school-board
Visitor, most teachers—and the principals who supervise
their classes—operate as if progressive education had not
proved the case for noise and freedom of bodily motion.
(Dewey stresses the salutary alternation of boisterous-
ness and tranquility.) The seats are no longer bolted to
the floor, but they still face front. Of course, the classes
are too large to cope with without "discipline." Then
make them smaller, or don't wonder if children escape
out of the cage, either into truancy or baffled daydream.
Here is a typical case: an architect replacing a Harlem
school is forbidden by the Board to spend money on
soundproofing the classrooms, even though the principal
has called it a necessity for the therapy of pent-up and
resentful children. The resentment, pent-up hostility,
is a major cause of reactive stupidity; yet there is usually
an absolute ban on overt expression of hostility, or even
of normal anger and aggression.

Again, one has to be blind not to see that, from the
onset of puberty, the dissidence from school is importantly sexual. Theoretically, the junior high school was
introduced to fit this change of life; yet astoundingly,
it is sexless. My own view, for what it's worth, is that
sexuality is lovely, there cannot be too much of it, it is
self-limiting if it is satisfactory, and satisfaction dimin-
ishes tension and clears the mind for attention and learning. Therefore, sexual expression should be approved in
and out of season, also in school, and where necessary
made the subject of instruction. But whether or not this
view is correct, it certainly is more practical than the

34

apparent attempt of the schools to operate as if sexual drives simply did not exist. When, on so crucial an issue, the schools act a hundred years out of date, they are crucially irrelevant.

But the following *is* something new:

"Trenton, May 24 (AP)—A state health official believes some overanxious New Jersey parents are dosing their children with tranquilizers before sending them to school ... the Health Department pediatrician assigned to the State Education Department said the parents apparently are trying to protect the children from cracking under pressure for good grades."

(d) Terrible damage is done to children simply by the size and standardization of the big system. Suppose a class size of 20 is good for average purposes; it does *not* follow that 35 is better than nothing. Rather, it is likely to be positively harmful, because the children have ceased to be persons and the teacher is destroyed as a teacher. A teacher with a 10-year-old class reading at 7-year level will have to use the content as well as the vocabulary of *Dick and Jane* since that is the textbook bought by the hundred thousands. The experience of a wise principal is that the most essential part of his job is to know every child's name and be an available "good father," so he wants a school for 400. Yet the city will build the school for 2000, because only that is practical, even though the essence is entirely dissipated. The chief part of learning is in the community of scholars, where classwork and social life may cohere; yet social engineers like Dr. Conant will, for putative efficiencies, centralize the high schools—the "enriched" curriculum with equipment is necessary for the national needs.

A program—e.g. to prevent drop-out—will be, by an attentive teacher, exquisitely tailored to the children he works with; he will have a success. Therefore his program must be standardized, watered down, for 75 schools —otherwise it cannot be financed—although now it is worthless. But here is an unbeatable anecdote: An architect is employed to replace a dilapidated school but is forbidden to consult the principal and teachers of the school about their needs, since his building must conform to uniform plans at headquarters, the plans being two generations out of date. As a functionalist, the architect demurs, and it requires an *ad hoc* assembly of all the superintendents to give him special permission.

Presumably all this is administratively necessary, but then it is aso necessary for bruised children to quit. Our society makes a persistent error in metaphysics. We are so mesmerized by the operation of a system with the appropriate name, for instance "Education," that we assume that it *must* be working somewhat, though admittedly not perfectly, when perhaps it has ceased to fulfill its function altogether and might even be preventing the function, for instance education.

(e) Especially today, when the hours of work will sharply diminish, the schools are supposed to educate for the satisfaction of life and for the worthwhile use of leisure. Again, let us try to be realistic, as a youngster

36

is. For most people, I think, a candid self-examination will show that their most absorbing, long, and satisfactory hours are spent in activities like friendly competitive sports, gambling, looking for love and love-making, earnest or argumentative conversation, political action with signs and sit-ins, solitary study and reading, contemplation of nature and cosmos, arts and crafts, music, and religion. Now none of these requires much money. Indeed, elaborate equipment takes the heart out of them. Friends use one another as resources. God, nature, and creativity are free. The media of the fine arts are cheap stuff. Health, luck, and affection are the only requirements for good sex. Good food requires taking pains more than spending money.

What is the moral for our purposes? Can it be denied that in some respects the drop-outs make a wiser choice than many who go to school, not to get real goods but to get money? Their choice of the "immediate"—their notorious "inability to tolerate delay"—is not altogether impulsive and neurotic. The bother is that in our present culture, which puts its entire emphasis on the consumption of expensive commodities, they are so nagged by inferiority, exclusion, and despair of the future that they cannot enjoy their leisure with a good conscience. Because they know little, they are deprived of many profound simple satisfactions and they never know what to do with themselves. Being afraid of exposing themselves to awkwardness and ridicule, they just hang around. And our urban social arrangements—e.g. high rent—have made it impossible for anybody to be decently poor on a "low" standard. One is either in the rat-race or has dropped out of society altogether.

(f) As a loyal academic, I must make a further observation. Mainly to provide Ph.D.'s, there is at present an overwhelming pressure to gear the "better" elementary schools to the graduate-universities. This is the great current reform, genre of Rickover. But what if the top of the ladder is corrupt and corrupts the lower grades? On visits to 70 colleges everywhere in the country, I have been appalled at how rarely the subjects are studied in a right academic spirit, for their truth and beauty and as part of humane international culture. The students are given, and seek, a narrow expertise, "mastery," aimed at licenses and salary. They are indoctrinated with a national thoughtlessness that is not even chauvinistic. Administrators sacrifice the community of scholars to aggrandizement and extramurally sponsored research.

Conversely, there is almost never conveyed the sense in which learning is truly practical, to enlighten experience, give courage to initiate and change, reform the state, deepen personal and social peace. On the contrary, the entire educational system itself creates professional cynicism or the resigned conviction that Nothing Can Be Done. If this is the University, how can we hope for aspiring scholarship in the elementary schools? On the contrary, everything will be grades and conforming, getting ahead not in the subject of interest but up the ladder. Students "do" Bronx Science in order to "make" M.I.T. and they "do" M.I.T. in order to "make" Westinghouse;

some of them have "done" Westinghouse in order to "make" jail.

## VI

What then? The compulsory system has become a universal trap, and it is no good. Very many of the youth, both poor and middle class, might be better off if the system simply did not exist, even if they then had no formal schooling at all. (I am extremely curious for a philosophic study of Prince Edward County in Virginia, where for some years schooling did not exist for Negro children.)

But what would become of these children? For very many, both poor and middle class, their homes are worse than the schools, and the city streets are worse in another way. Our urban and suburban environments are precisely not cities or communities where adults naturally attend to the young and educate to a viable life. Also, perhaps especially in the case of the overt drop-outs, the state of their body and soul is such that we must give them refuge and remedy, whether it be called school, settlement house, youth worker, or work camp.

There are thinkable alternatives. Throughout this little book, as occasion arises, I shall offer alternative proposals that I as a single individual have heard of or thought up. Here are half a dozen directly relevant to the subject we have been discussing, the system as compulsory trap. In principle, when a law begins to do more harm than good, the best policy is to alleviate it or try doing without it.

i. Have "no school at all" for a few classes. These children should be selected from tolerable, though not necessarily cultured, homes. They should be neighbors and numerous enough to be a society for one another and so that they do not feel merely "different." Will they learn the rudiments anyway? This experiment cannot do the children any academic harm, since there is good evidence that normal children will make up the first seven years school-work with four to seven months of good teaching.

ii. Dispense with the school building for a few classes; provide teachers and use the city itself as the school—its streets, cafeterias, stores, movies, museums, parks, and factories. Where feasible, it certainly makes more sense to teach using the real subject-matter than to bring an abstraction of the subject-matter into the school-buiding as "curriculum." Such a class should probably not exceed 10 children for one pedagogue. The idea—it is the model of Athenian education—is not dissimilar to Youth gang work, but not applied to delinquents and not playing to the gang ideology.

iii. Along the same lines, but both outside and inside the school building, use appropriate *unlicensed* adults of the community—the druggist, the storekeeper, the mechanic—as the proper educators of the young into the grown-up world. By this means we can try to overcome the separation of the young from the grown-up world so characteristic in modern urban life, and to diminish the omnivorous authority of the professional school-people. Certainly it would be a useful and animating experience for the adults. (There is the beginning of such a volunteer program in the New York and some other systems.)

iv. Make class attendance not compulsory, in the manner of A. S. Neill's Summerhill. If the teachers are good, absence would tend to be eliminated; if they are bad, let them know it. The compulsory law is useful to get the children away from the parents, but it must not result in trapping the children. A fine modification of this suggestion is the rule used by Frank Brown in Florida: he permits the children to be absent for a week or a month to engage in any worthwhile enterprise or visit any new environment.

v. Decentralize an urban school (or do not build a new big building) into small units, 20 to 50, in available store-fronts or clubhouses. These tiny schools, equipped with record-player and pin-ball machine, could combine play, socializing, discussion, and formal teaching. For special events, the small units can be brought together into a common auditorium or gymnasium, so as to give the sense of the greater community. Correspondingly, I think it would be worthwhile to give the Little Red Schoolhouse a spin under modern urban conditions, and see how it works out: that is, to combine all the ages in a little room for 25 to 30, rather than to grade by age.

vi. Use a pro rata part of the school money to send

children to economically marginal farms for a couple of months of the year, perhaps 6 children from mixed backgrounds to a farmer. The only requirement is that the farmer feed them and not beat them; best, of course, if they take part in the farm-work. This will give the farmer cash, as part of the generally desirable program to redress the urban-rural ratio to something nearer to 70% to 30%. (At present, less than 8% of families are rural.) Conceivably, some of the urban children will take to the other way of life, and we might generate a new kind of rural culture.

I frequently suggest these and similar proposals at teachers colleges, and I am looked at with an eerie look— do I really mean to *diminish* the state-aid grant for each student-day? But mostly the objection is that such proposals entail intolerable administrative difficulties.

Above all, we must apply these or any other proposals to particular individuals and small groups, without the obligation of uniformity. There is a case for uniform standards of achievement, lodged in the Regents, but they *cannot* be reached by uniform techniques. The claim that standardization of procedure is more efficient, less costly, or alone administratively practical, is often false. Particular inventiveness requires thought, but thought does not cost money.

# 2

# Visiting
# a school

## I

Leading a seminar in the philosophy of Education—
it was at Antioch—I was met by the point-blank question:
"What would you say is the chief use of the elementary
schools?" After a moment, I found myself blurting out,
"Why, I suppose it's to undo the damage done at home,
so the child can begin to breathe again and be curious."
At this the student-teachers laughed and asked what
was the purpose of high school. I had to answer, of
course, "To undo the damage done by the elementary
schools." And any one who has had the misfortune of
teaching college freshmen will agree that the chief aim
of at least the freshman year in college is to try and undo

some of the damage done by the high schools. No doubt, the chief purpose of the school of hard knocks is to undo the effects of the colleges. But perhaps, in our highly interlocked society, it's all of a piece.

We can look at it the other way and say that the chief purpose of the elementary schools is to relieve the home, to baby-sit. But it is such an expensive kind of baby-sitting!—it costs annually $650 a child in a New York City grade school, about $1000 in high school.

## II

What kind of alternative environment to the home does the school in fact give? What is its animal and moral tone? Let me describe a school Visit. (West Side of Manhattan, predominantly a Puerto Rican area.)

It was a luckily small class—I counted less than 20 —exceptional in the New York system where the classes run to 35 and more, though the technical "average" is 29. The lesson was on Weather, and what the teacher wanted was to get them to say that temperature varies with altitude, latitude, and season. She intended to write these words on the board, and that's what she was after. She was not a bad gal, but a poor teacher. She did not ask about the weather in Puerto Rico, where several had undoubtedly been.

But the salient condition in that class was that every

few moments—during the 40 minutes I sat there, about 10 times—she said, "Now speak louder! I can't hear. Louder!" And she repeated her question on latitude and altitude. It was obvious enough that the foreground object, which in fact demanded pedagogy, was that the children were muffled. They sat in a dejected posture, and they could not, physically could not, throw out their voices. Psychosomatically, they could not then have a very aggressive attitude toward the subject-matter either, toward grasping it, taking it in.

One expedient would have been to go close to the kid and say, "Sit up, young lady, and breathe from the diaphragm. Here, where I'm touching you. You aren't using these muscles. See, if I press your ribs they hurt. Now move your bottom ribs here—that's the diaphragm, and throw *out* your breath and shout . . . What should you shout? Just shout Shout!" If she had done that, the children would very soon have been able to throw their voices; they would have been breathing better; some of them might have gotten a little dizzy. They would also soon have had a more aggressive attitude toward the lesson.

It happened in that school, however, that the principal was a little of a maniac on noise. He had instituted silent passing in the halls. He explained to me that the Puerto Rican children were very wild; if he let them talk to one another between classes, they soon became boisterous, and then ten minutes of the class time was spent in calming them down. They were calmed down only too well, for the 40 minutes of every hour.

While I was talking with him, there was a petty noise in the hall. He jumped out of his skin and rushed with angry shouts, to find who had made that noise. Clearly, if the teacher had had the kids shout, a supervisor would have descended on her, and she would have had something to answer for.

All right, one went into the shop class, where there was some noise. But here was a kid who couldn't hammer a nail; he missed, or he controlled the swing and only tapped. The teacher did nothing about it. But it seemed to me that the way the kid kept his shoulders tense—perhaps against letting out hostility—he *couldn't* hammer, any more than he could throw a punch. The important thing in a seventh grade shop-class is not for the kid to make a box, but for him to do it with force and grace, to become an amateur carpenter, and then he might make fine boxes. Would not a good teacher work on this specifically, on force and grace and the emotional inhibiting of motor execution?

In the gym they were doing the President's push-ups, ordained by John Kennedy who was eager to have the youth physically fit. Apparently, physical fitness was going to be achieved by the ability to do certain calisthenic exercises; or at least it would be measured by the exercises—the teacher would have something to write down. The children were doing the prescribed number of push-ups, the prescribed number of chin-ups. In fact, three quarters of the class were faking the chin-up outrageously (just as I always did), elbows rigid, holding breath, but making like they had done the exercise. In a few cases, this was probably positively damaging, straining; in most cases, the business was a perfunctory proof performance, meaning "O.K., let me alone." In some cases, it would be part of a distaste and shame for the use of one's body altogether, not giving in to the physical effort.

It seems to me that the authentic methods for elementary physical education—but of course no normal schools are teaching such methods—are eurhythmics and what the psychologists call Character Analysis, the training of emotion, and the liberation of inhibited emotion, by psychosomatic and muscular behavior. The problem of each of these children is that he is unable to express his anger, his grief, his sexuality. Yet nothing is done to unblock the fear of expression, of body contact, of nakedness. There is a kind of music-teaching, but it does not seek to draw on actual feeling and to integrate feeling by rhythm and harmony.

Rather amusingly, this same school happened to have an extra-curricular activity, social dancing, with the children as drummers, initiated by a lively young woman teacher. Dancing their cha-cha, the children were marvelous little acrobats, with plenty of grace and force and intricate rhythms that would have delighted Dalcroze. They had no need of the President's exercises at all. I Calvinistically thought it was a pity that they were not also learning to notate all this and go on to composition—but that no doubt would have spoiled it.

## III

What, realistically, was a member of Local Board 6 & 8 to advise, as a result of that Visit? Suppose that the gym teacher, or the shop teacher, or the teacher of meteorology *did* pursue a proper educational course. Without doubt, in some cases there would be a great outburst of dammed up hostility, and plenty of tears. A child might go home and tell off his father. He might even tell off the teacher. The expression of that hostility—and even more, the expression of grief or sexual desire—might lead to the most horrendous consequences. The church would complain. The newspapers, that thrive on pornography and murder, would surely note with alarm. The Mayor would be called on. And the teacher would very soon be fired. Nor—my guess is—would the Teachers Union come to the rescue.

But the children might get over their retroflected rage and shame, relax their reactive stupidity (almost all stupidity is a "defense"), and find themselves again in a *possible* environment.

# 3

# The present moment
# in progressive
# education

I

The program of progressive education always antici-
pates the crucial social problems that everybody will be
concerned with a generation later, when it is too late for
the paradisal solutions of progressive educators. This is
in the nature of the case. Essentially, progressive education is nothing but the attempt to naturalize, to humanize,
each new social and technical development that is making
traditional education irrelevant. It is not a reform of
education, but a reconstruction in terms of the new era.
If society would *once* adopt this reconstruction, we
could at last catch up with ourselves and grow naturally
into the future. But equally in the nature of the case,

society rejects, half-accepts, bastardizes the necessary changes; and so we are continually stuck with "unfinished revolutions," as I called them in *Growing Up Absurd*. Then occur the vast social problems that *could* have been avoided—that indeed the older progressive education had specifically addressed—but it is too late. And progressive educators stoically ask, What is the case *now?*

During the current incredible expansion of increasingly unnatural schooling, and increasing alienation of the young, it is useful to trace the course of progressive education in this century, from John Dewey to the American version of A. S. Neill.

## II

The recent attacks on Deweyan progressive education, by the Rickovers and Max Raffertys, have really been outrageous—one gets impatient. Historically, the intent of Dewey was exactly the opposite of what the critics say. Progressive education appeared in this country in the intellectual, moral, and social crisis of the development of big centralized industrialism after the Civil War. It was the first thoroughgoing modern analysis of the crucial modern problem of every advanced country in the world: how to cope with high industrialism and scientific technology which are strange to people; how to restore competence to people who are becoming ignorant; how to live in the rapidly growing cities so that they will not be mere urban sprawl; how to have a free society in mass conditions; how to make the high industrial system good for something, rather than a machine running for its own sake.

That is, progressive education was the correct solution of a real problem that Rickover is concerned with, the backwardness of people in a scientific world. To put it more accurately, if progressive education had been generally adopted, we should not be so estranged and ignorant today.

The thought of John Dewey was part of a similar tendency in architecture, the functionalism of Louis Sullivan and Frank Lloyd Wright, that was trying to invent an urbanism and an esthetic suited to machine-production and yet human; and it went with the engineering orientation of the economic and moral theory of Veblen. These thinkers wanted to train, teach—perhaps accustom is the best word—the new generation to the actualities of industrial and technical life, working practically with the machinery, learning by doing. People could then be at home in the modern world, and possibly become free.

At-homeness had also a political aspect. Dewey was distressed by both the robber-baron plutocracy and the bossed mass-democracy; and he was too wise to espouse Veblen's technocracy, engineer's values. Dewey put a good deal of faith in industrial democracy, overestimating the labor movement—he did not foresee the bureaucratization of the unions. As a pragmatist he probably expected that the skilled would become initiators in management and production; he did not foresee that labor demands would diminish to wages and working conditions.

But the school, he felt, could combine all the necessary elements: practical learning of science and technology, democratic community, spontaneous feeling liberated by artistic appreciation, freedom to fantasize, and animal expression freed from the parson's morality and the schoolmaster's ruler. This constituted the whole of Deweyan progressive education. There would be spontaneous interest (including animal impulse), harmonized by art-working; this spontaneity would be controlled by the hard pragmatism of doing and making the doing actually work; and thus the young democratic community would learn the modern world and also have the will to change it. Progressive education was a theory of continual scientific experiment and orderly, nonviolent social revolution.

As was inevitable, this theory was entirely perverted when it began to be applied, either in private schools or in the public system. The conservatives and the businessmen cried out, and the program was toned down. The practical training and community democracy, whose purpose was to live scientifically and change society, was changed into "socially useful" subjects and a psychology of "belonging." In our schools, driver-training survives as the type of the "useful." (By now, I suspect, Dewey would have been urging us to curtail the number of cars.) Social-dancing was the type of the "belonging." The

Americans had no intention of broadening the scientific base and taking technological expertness and control out of the hands of the top managers and their technicians. And democratic community became astoundingly interpreted as conformity, instead of being the matrix of social experiment and political change.

## III

Curiously, just in the past few years, simultaneous with the attack on "Dewey," his ideas have been getting most prestigious official endorsement (though they are not attributed to Dewey). In the great post-Sputnik cry to increase the scientific and technical pool, the critics of "Dewey" call for strict lessons and draconian grading and weeding-out (plus bribes), to find the élite group. (Dr. Conant says that the "academically talented" are 15% and these, selected by national tests, will be at home *for* us in the modern technical world as its creative spirits.) However, there is an exactly contrary theory, propounded by the teachers of science, e.g. the consensus of the Woods Hole Conference of the National Science Foundation, reported in Professor Bruner's *The Processes of Education*. This theory counsels practical learning by doing, entirely rejects competition and grading, and encourages fantasy and guesswork. There is no point, it claims, in learning the "answers," for very soon

53

there will be different answers. Rather, what must be taught are the underlying ideas of scientific thought, continuous with the substance of the youngster's feelings and experience. In short, the theory is Deweyan progressive education.

To be sure, Professor Bruner and his associates do not go on to espouse democratic community. But I am afraid they will eventually find that also this is essential, for it is impossible to do creative work of any kind when the goals are pre-determined by outsiders and cannot be criticized and altered by the minds that have to do the work, even if they are youngsters. (Dewey's principle is, simply, that good teaching is that which leads the student to want to learn something more.)

The compromise of the National Science Foundation on this point is rather comical. "Physical laws are not asserted; they are, it is hoped, discovered by the student"; "there is a desire to allow each student to experience some of the excitement that scientific pursuits afford"—I am quoting from the NSF's *Science Course Improvement Projects*. That is, the student is to make a leap of discovery to—what is already known, in a course precharted by the Ph.D.'s at M.I.T. Far from being elating, such a process must be profoundly disappointing; my guess is that the "discovery" will be greeted not by a cheer but by a razz. The excitement of discovery is reduced to the animation of puzzle-solving. I doubt that puzzle-solving is what creative thought is about, though it is certainly what many Ph.D.'s are about.

54

## IV

Authentic progressive education, meantime, has moved into new territory altogether, how to cope with the over-centralized organization and Organization Men of our society, including the top-down direction of science by the National Science Foundation. The new progressive theory is "Summerhill."

The American Summerhill movement is modeling itself on A. S. Neill's school in England, but with significant deviations—so that Neill does not want his name associated with some of the offshoots.

Like Dewey, Neill stressed free animal expression, learning by doing, and *very* democratic community processes (one person one vote, enfranchising small children!). But he also asserted a principle that to Dewey did not seem important, the freedom to choose to go to class or stay away altogether. A child at Summerhill can just hang around; he'll go to class when he damned well feels like it—and some children, coming from compulsory schools, don't damned well feel like it for eight or nine months. But after a while, as the curiosity in the soul revives— and since their friends go—they give it a try.

It is no accident, as I am trying to show in this book, that it is just *this* departure in progressive education that is catching on in America, whereas most of the surviving Deweyan schools are little better than the good suburban schools that imitated them. The advance-guard problem is that the compulsory school system, like the whole of our economy, politics, and standard of living, has become a lockstep. It is no longer designed for the maximum growth and future practical utility of the children into a changing world, but is inept social engineering for extrinsic goals, pitifully short-range. Even when it is benevolent, it is in the bureaucratic death-grip of a uniformity of conception, from the universities down, that cannot possibly suit the multitude of dispositions and conditions. Yet 100% of the children are supposed to remain for at least 12 years in one kind of box; and of course those who attend private Deweyan schools are being aimed for 4 to 8 years more. Thus, if we are going to experiment with real universal education that educates, we have to start by getting rid of compulsory schooling altogether.

## V

One American variant of Summerhill has developed in a couple of years in an unforeseen direction. Like Summerhill this school is not urban, but, unlike Summerhill, it is not residential. Many of the children come from a nearby colony of artists, some of them of international fame. The artist parents, and other parents, come into the school as part-time teachers, of music, painting, building, dancing.

Being strong-minded, they, and the regular teachers, soon fell out with the headmaster, the founder, who had been a Summerhill teacher; they stripped him of important prerogatives and he resigned. Inevitably other parents had to join in the discussions and decisions, on real and difficult issues. The result seems to have been the formation of a peculiar kind of extended family, unified by educating the children, and incorporating a few professional teachers. But meantime, imitated from Neill, there is the democratic council, in which the children have a very loud voice and an equal vote, and this gives them an institutional means to communicate with, and get back at, their parents. It is stormy and factional. Some parents have pulled out and teachers have quit. Yet, inadvertently, there is developing a brilliant solution to crucial problems of American life: how can children grow up in live contact with many adults; how can those who do the work run the show; how to transcend a rigid professionalism that is wasteful of human resources.

At present one of the teachers at this school is preparing to try out a little Summerhill school in a slum area in New York.

Another Summerhill variant has taken a different course: to use the school almost directly as social action. To overcome the artificial stratification of modern society, it brings together not only Negroes and whites but delinquents and the well-behaved. Naturally this gets the school into trouble with its surroudings. It has had to flee from the South to the North, and it is in trouble again in the North.

Such a combination of education and direct social action is springing up on all sides. The so-called Northern

Student Movement is a group of college-students who take a year off from college to tutor urban underprivileged kids referred by the public schools; but the NSM has now declared as its policy *not* to restrict itself to the curriculum and aims of the school system. The Student Non-Violent Coordinating Committee is about—I am writing in June 1964—to go down to the deep South, primarily to help in the voter-registration of disenfranchised Negroes, but also to try out little colleges for adolescents, with 5 graduate-students teaching 25 teenagers a curriculum relevant to their economic and political advancement. Accompanying the numerous school-boycotts there have sprung up "Freedom" schools that started as one-day propaganda demonstrations but have been lively enough to warrant continuing.

In my opinion, the highly official Peace Corps has the same underlying educational significance. At present it is rigidly selective and super-collegiate; indeed it is, by and large, an operation for upper-middle class youth and well-paid professors and administrators: it costs $15,-000 to get one youngster in the field for a year. Nevertheless, the whole conception is unthinkable except as dissatisfaction with orthodox schooling and with the status-careers that that schooling leads to.

## VI

The future—if we survive and have a future, which is touch and go—will certainly be more leisurely. If that leisure is not to be completely inane and piggishly affluent, there must be a community and civic culture. There must be more employment in human services and less in the production of hardware gadgets; more citizenly initiative and less regimentation; and in many spheres, decentralization of control and administration. For these purposes, the top-down dictated national plans and educational methods that are now the fad are quite irrelevant. And on the contrary, it is precisely the society of free choice, lively engagement, and social action of Summerhill and American Summerhill that are relevant and practical.

Thus, just as with Dewey, the new advance of progressive education is a good index of what the real situation is. And no doubt society will again seek to abuse this program which it needs but is afraid of.

# Part two

# *High School*

# 4

# A proposal
# to extend
# compulsory
# schooling

## I

In an address to the American Bankers Association
on February 24, 1964, the Secretary of Labor proposed
to *extend* compulsory schooling to the age of 18. This
at a time when in New York a Kings County Grand Jury
proposed *reducing* it to 15 and giving the superintendent
of schools leeway to kick out the unruly. In many schools
in the country policeman are stationed to keep guard
over youngsters who do not want to be there. And the
majority of drop-outs who were cajoled into returning

to school in 1963 soon dropped out again, since nothing essential had been changed in purpose, method, or curriculum; they only suffered a new humiliation by being conned. And—*verb. sat. sap.*—older lads tend to be heavier and to carry more powerful armament. Did the Secretary of Labor think it through?

In some places, e.g. Milwaukee, the compulsory age is at present 18, on the following arrangement: if, after 16, a youngster has a job, he goes to Continuation School (Milwaukee Vocational) one day a week; if he has no job, he attends full time, till 18. How does this work out? An administrator of the school tells me, "We don't teach them anything, neither academic subjects nor a trade. They're ineducable, and there aren't any jobs for them to train for anyway. But we do try to improve their attitude. Of course, we usually only have them for about 7 months."

"Why? What happens to them?"

"Oh, they join the Army or end up in Wales"— Wales is the reform school.

Naturally I become indignant and say, "What would become of *your* attitude if I caged you in a schoolroom and didn't even attempt to teach you anything? Wouldn't it be better to go to an honest jail?" But these angry questions do not seem to flurry him at all. Obviously I am not in touch with the concrete realities of his situation.

## II

In his address, Secretary Wirtz makes the usual correlation between employment and years of schooling: "The unemployment rate for individuals today with less than 5 years of school is 10.4 percent. For those with 9 to 11 years of school, it is 7.8 percent; for those with 13 to 15 years of school, 4 percent; but for those with 16 or more years of school, the unemployment rate drops to 1.4 percent."

But these figures are unimpressive. As he himself implies in another context, the *prima facie* explanation of the correlation is the parents' income: By connections, manners and aspirations, middle-class children get middle-class jobs; schooling is an incidental part of it. Lower-class children used to get lower-class jobs, but just these jobs have petered out; in the present *structure* of the economy, the money and jobs do not filter down. Similarly, the docility, neatness of appearance, etc. that are useful for getting petty jobs, are not created by years of schooling but they are accurately measured by them. In my opinion, the same line of criticism strongly applies to the spectacular correlations between life-time income and years of schooling. Looking for his first job, a middle class youth decides he wants $80 to start, and he can afford to shop around till he gets it; a poor boy must take anything and starts at $35. For obvious reasons, this initial difference will usually predetermine the whole career. Conversely, a sharp poor boy, seeing that this is the score, might choose not to bestir himself and prefer to look for a racket.

Again, Negro college graduates average in a lifetime the same salary as white high school graduates. It seems to be *not* the years of schooling but the whole context that makes the difference. Consider. If after seven or eight years, the salary increase of Negro or Puerto Rican high school graduates over those who have dropped out is perhaps $5 a week, is this worth the painful effort of years of schooling that is intrinsically worthless and spirit-breaking?

In these circumstances, it is wiser to think exactly the opposite way. It would probably help to improve the educational aspiration and educability of poor youngsters to give the money to poor families *directly*, rather than to channel it through school systems or other social agencies that drain off most of it for the same middle-class. If we pension the poor as consumers in a consumption-oriented society, they will also send their children to school, a form of consumption. I take it that this is what Galbraith and Theobald are essentially saying. And the proposals of Myrdal and Keyserling are meant to accomplish the same purpose: public works to provide *unskilled* jobs.

III

It is claimed that society needs more people who are technically trained. But informed labor people tell me

66

that, for a job requiring skill but no great genius, a worker can be found at once, or quickly trained, to fill it. For instance, the average job in General Motors' most automated plant requires three weeks of training for those who have no education whatever. It used to require six weeks; for such jobs, automation has diminished rather than increased the need for training. In the Army and Navy, fairly complicated skills, e.g. radar operation and repair, are taught in a year *on the job*, often to practical illiterates.

Naturally, if diplomas are pre-requisite to hiring a youngster, the correlation of schooling and employment is self-proving. Because of this fad, there is a fantastic amount of mis-hiring, hiring young people far too school-trained for the routine jobs they get. I was struck by a recent report in the *Wall Street Journal* of firms philanthropically deciding to hire *only* drop-outs for certain categories of jobs, since the diploma made no difference in performance.

Twist it and turn it how you will, there is no logic to the proposal to extend compulsory schooling *except* as a device to keep the unemployed off the streets by putting them into concentration camps called schools. The Continuation branch of Milwaukee Vocational is, then, typical of what we can expect. (By the way, Milwaukee Vocational is otherwise a justly famous school, a fine product of Populism and right-wing Socialism.)

As an academic, I am appalled by this motivation for schooling. As a citizen and human being, I am appalled by this waste of youthful vitality. It is time that we stopped using the word "education" honorifically. We must ask, education how? where? for what? and under whose administration? Certainly every youth should get the best possible education, but, in my opinion, the present kind of compulsory schooling under the present administrators, far from being extended, should be sharply curtailed.


# IV


As I have been saying, by and large primary schooling is, and should be, mainly baby-sitting. It has the great mission of democratic socialization—it certainly must not be segregated by race and income; apart from this, it should be happy, interesting, not damaging. The noise about stepping-up the primary curriculum is quite uncalled for; I have seen no convincing evidence—not by progressive educators either—that early schooling makes much academic difference in the long run. But in the secondary schools, after puberty, the tone of the baby-sitting must necessarily turn to regimentation and policing, and it is at peril that we require schooling; it fits some, it hurts others. A recent study by Edgar Friedenberg concludes that spirit-breaking is the *principal* function of typical lower middle-class schools.

I wonder whether the Secretary of Labor thought through the constitutionality, not to speak of the morals, of his compulsory proposal. The legal justifications for compulsory schooling have been to protect children from exploitation by parents and employers, and to ensure the basic literacy and civics necessary for a democratic electorate. It is quite a different matter to deprive adolescents of their freedom in order to alleviate the difficulties of a faulty economic and political system. Is this constitutional?

We are back, in another context, to Dr. Conant's intolerable distinction between "individual development" and "national needs"; Dr. Conant was talking about the post-Sputnik putative need for scientists, Secretary Wirtz was talking about unemployment. So let us go over the ground again and look at the picture squarely. At present, in most states, for 10 to 13 years every young person is obliged to sit the better part of his day in a room almost always too crowded, facing front, doing lessons predetermined by a distant administration at the state capital and that have no relation to his own intellectual, social, or animal interests, and not much relation even to his economic interests. The overcrowding precludes individuality or spontaneity, reduces the young to ciphers, and the teacher to a martinet. If a youth tries to follow his own bent, he is interrupted and even jailed. If he does not perform, he is humiliated and threatened, but he is *not allowed to fail and get out*. Middle class youth go through this for at least four more years—at the college level, the overcrowding has become an academic scandal—but they are steeled to it and supported by their middle-class anxiety and middle-class perquisites, including money to spend. Secretary Wirtz now wants poor youth, not thus steeled and supported, to get two more years of it. What will this 17-year-old do for spending money?

In his speech the Secretary referred to the admirable extension of free education from 1850 to, say, 1930. But this is again entirely misleading with regard to our present situation. To repeat, that opening of opportunity took place in an open economy, with an expanding market for skills and cultural learning. Young people took advantage of it *of their own volition;* therefore there were no blackboard jungles and endemic problems of discipline. Teachers taught those who wanted to learn; therefore there was no especial emphasis on grading. What is the present situation? The frantic competitive testing and grading means that the market for skills and learning is *not* open, it is tight. There are relatively few employers for those who score high; and almost none of the high-scorers become independent enterprisers. This means, in effect, that a few great corporations are getting the benefit of an enormous weeding-out and selective process—all children are fed into the mill and everybody pays for it.

If our present high schools, junior colleges, and colleges reflected the desire, freedom, and future of opportunity of the young, there would be no grading, no testing except as a teaching method, and no blackboard jungles. In fact, we are getting lockstep scheduling and grading to the point of torture. The senior year of high school is sacrificed to batteries of national tests, and policemen are going to stand in the corridors. Even an élite school such as Bronx Science—singled out by Dr. Conant as the best school in the country—is run as if for delinquents, with corridor passes and a ban on leaving the building. The conclusion is inevitable: The scholastically bright are not following their aspirations but are being pressured and bribed; the majority—those who are bright but not scholastic, and those who are not especially bright but have other kinds of vitality—are being subdued.

## V

This is the schooling that Secretary Wirtz says we "ought to make the biggest industry in the country." I thought it already was! As one observes the sprawling expansion of the universities and colleges, eating up their neighborhoods, dislocating the poor, dictating to the lower schools, battening on Federal billions for research and development, and billions for buildings, and billions through the National Defense Education Act, and billions from foundations and endowments—one suddenly realizes that here again is the Dead Hand of the medieval church, that inherits and inherits and never dies. The University, which should be dissident and poor, has become the Establishment. The streets are full of its monks.

What a bad scene! Its spirit pervades all of society. Let me quote from a man in Secretary Wirtz's own department, in charge of retraining: "We retrain him, but before the course is finished, that job too has vanished. So we begin again. But after the fourth or fifth retraining, he has a job that doesn't vanish: he becomes a Teacher of Retraining." We must remember that, whatever the motive, *pouring money into the school-and-college system and into the academic social-work way of coping with problems, is strictly class legislation that confirms the inequitable structure of the economy.* I have mentioned how the professor-ridden Peace Corps needs $15,000 to get a single youngster in the field for a year, whereas the dedicated Quakers achieve almost the same end for $3,500. Again, when $13 millions are allotted for a local Mobilization for Youth program, it is soon found that nearly $12 millions have gone for sociologists doing "research," diplomated social workers, the N.Y. school system, and administrators, but only one million to field workers and the youths themselves.

## VI

In my opinion, the public buys this unexamined "education" because of the following contradiction: The Americans are guilty because these youth *are* useless in the present set-up, so they spend money on them (though they get oddly stingy at crucial moments); on the other hand, they insist that the youth work hard at something

72

"useful"—namely useless training. One can't just let them play ball; they must compete and suffer.

I agree that we ought to spend more public money on education. And where jobs exist and there is need for technical training, the corporations ought to spend more money on apprenticeships. We are an affluent society and can afford it. And the conditions of modern life are far too complicated for independent young spirits to get going on their own. They need some preparation, though probably not as much as is supposed; but more important, they need various institutional frameworks in which they can try out and learn the ropes.

Nevertheless, I would not give a penny more to the present school administrators. The situation is this: to make the present school set-up even *tolerable*, not positively damaging—e.g. to cut the elementary class size to 20 or to provide colleges enough to diminish the frantic competition for places—will require at least *doubling* the present school budgets. I submit that this kind of money should be spent in other ways.

# VII

What, then, ought the education of these youth to be? We are back to our fundamental question: what are the alternatives?

Fundamentally, there is no right education except

73

growing up into a worthwhile world. Indeed, our excessive concern with problems of education at present simply means that the grown-ups do not have such a world. The poor youth of America will *not* become equal by rising through the middle class, going to middle-class schools. By plain social justice, the Negroes and other minorities have the right to, and must get, equal opportunity for schooling with the rest, but the exaggerated expectation from the schooling is a chimera—and, I fear, will be shockingly disappointing. But also the middle-class youth will not escape their increasing exploitation and *anomie* in such schools. A decent education aims at, prepares for, a more worthwhile future, with a different community spirit, different occupations, and more real utility than attaining status and salary.

We are suffering from a bad style, perhaps a wrong religion. Although it is pretty certain, as I have said, that the automated future will see less employment in the manufacture of hardware and more employment in service occupations, as well as more leisure, yet astoundingly the mass-production and cash-accounting attitude toward the hardware is carried over unchanged into the thinking about the services and leisure! The lockstep regimentation and the petty-bourgeois credits and competitive grading in the schooling are typical of all the rest. (For a charming, and grim, study of the spread of "business methods" to schooling, from 1900 to 1930, let me refer the reader to Callahan's *The Cult of Efficiency in American Education*.)

My bias is that we should maximize automation as

74

quickly as possible, *where it is relevant*—taking care to cushion job dislocation and to provide adequate social insurance. But the spirit and method of automation, logistics, chain of command, and clerical work are *entirely irrelevant* to humane services, community service, communications, community culture, high culture, citizenly initiative, education, and recreation. To give a rather special but not trivial example of what I mean, TV sets should be maximum-mass-produced with maximum automation, in a good standard model, as cheaply as possible; but TV programming should, except for a few national services, be as much decentralized, tailor-made, and reliant on popular and free-artist initiative as possible.

The dangers of the highly technological and automated future are obvious: We might become a brainwashed society of idle and frivolous consumers. We might continue in a rat race of highly competitive, unnecessary busy-work with a meaninglessly expanding Gross National Product. In either case, there might still be an out-cast group that must be suppressed. To countervail these dangers and make active, competent, and initiating citizens who can produce a community culture and a noble recreation, we need a very different education than the schooling that we have been getting.

Large parts of it must be directly useful, rather than useless and merely aiming at status. Here we think of the spending in the public sector, advocated by Myrdal, Keyserling, Galbraith, and many others. E.g. the money spent on town improvement, community service, or rural rehabilitation can also provide educational occasions.

75

(When these economists invariably list schooling as high
—and often first—in the list of public expenditures, they
fail to realize that such expense is probably wasted and
perhaps even further dislocates the economy. I would
say the same about Galbraith's pitch for new highways.)

On the whole, the education must be voluntary
rather than compulsory, for no growth to freedom occurs except by intrinsic motivation. Therefore the educational opportunities must be various and variously ad-
ministered. We must diminish rather than expand the
present monolithic school system. I would suggest that,
on the model of the GI-Bill, we experiment, giving the
school money directly to the high-school age adolescents,
for any plausible self-chosen educational proposals, such
as purposeful travel or individual enterprise. This would
also, of course, lead to the proliferation of experimental
schools.

Unlike the present inflexible lockstep, our educational policy must allow for periodic quitting and easy
return to the scholastic ladder, so that the young have
time to find themselves and to study when they are themselves ready. This is Eric Erickson's valuable notion of
the need for *moratoria* in the life-career; and the anthro-
pological insistence of Stanley Diamond and others, that
our society neglects the crises of growing up.

Education must foster independent thought and expression, rather than conformity. For example, to countervail the mass communications, we have an imperative
social need, indeed a constitutional need to protect liberty, for many thousands of independent media: local

newspapers, independent broadcasters, little magazines, little theaters; and these, under professional guidance, could provide remarkable occasions for the employment and education of adolescents of brains and talent. (I have elsewhere proposed a graduated tax on the audience-size of mass-media, to provide a Fund to underwrite such new independent ventures for a period, so that they can try to make their way.)

Finally, contemporary education must inevitably be heavily weighted toward the sciences. But this does not necessarily call for school-training of a relatively few technicians, or rare creative scientists (if such can indeed be trained in schools). Our aim must be to make a great number of citizens at home in a technological environ- ment, not alienated from the machines we use, not igno- rant as consumers, who can somewhat judge govern- mental scientific policy, who can enjoy the humanistic beauty of the sciences, and, above all, who can under- stand the morality of a scientific way of life. I try to spell out the meaning of this below. (See Chapter 7).

When Secretary Wirtz means by education some- thing like this, and not compulsory junior college for delinquents, we can think of extending education as a device for diminishing youth unemployment. Because it will then be more useful employment than most of the available, or non-available, jobs. It will be relevant to a good future rather than a morally-bankrupt past.

# 5

# The universe
# of discourse
# in which
# they grow up

## I

Let us now consider the interaction of school and the general culture as a climate of communication and ask:

What happens to the language and thought of young Americans as they grow up toward and through adolescence?

In the institutional speech, a child hears only one world-view. In the nature of the case, every mass-medium caters to a big common-denominator of opinion and taste, but even more influential is that the mass-media interlock. "News," for instance, is what is selected as newsworthy by two or three news-services; three almost identical broadcasting networks abstract from the same; and the same is again abridged for the *Junior Scholastic*. Even for this news, only 60 towns in America now have competing newspapers (in 1900 there were 600). Similarly, the "standard of living," the way to live respectably and decently, is what is shown in the ads in a few mass-circulation magazines and identically in the TV commercials. Movie-sets of respectable life come from the same kind of engineers. Similarly, "political thought" is the platforms of two major parties that agree on all crucial issues, like the Cold War and the Expanding Economy, and that get practically all of the coverage by the same newspapers and broadcasters.

Much of this public speech is quite meaningless. The ads compete with high rhetoric but the commodities are nearly the same, and a child can see that our lives are not *quite* so vastly occupied by soap, cigarettes, and beer. Politicians are very polemical, but they avoid any concrete issues that might differentiate the candidates and lose votes. The real meaning of the speeches, the goal of profits and power, is never stated. By age 11 or 12, bright children, perhaps readers of *Mad* magazine, recognize that most of the speech is mere words.

The interlocking of the schools into the system is more serious, for here the children have to work at it and cooperate. The story is the same. The galloping increase of national tests guarantee that the class-work will become nothing but preparation for these same tests. Corporation talent-scouts hover in the high schools, and even the primary schools are flooded with corporation brochures. Excellent scientists in Washington who chart courses in science and mathematics understand that there must be leeway for individuality and guesswork; but in the hands of incompetent teachers, the national standard naturally becomes an inflexible ruler. And TV and machine-teaching are formal statements that *everybody apperceives in the same way, with no need for dialogue.*

Apart from family, children have little speech with any adults except schoolteachers. But the crowding and scheduling in school allow little chance or time for personal contact. Also, increasingly in grade schools as well as in colleges, the teachers have abdicated their personal role to specialist counsellors and administrators, so that confiding and guidance tend to occur only in extreme situations. One must be "deviant" to be attended to as a human being.

This public speech cannot easily be tested against direct observation or experience. Urban and suburban children do not see crafts and industries. Playthings are prefabricated toys; there is little practical carpentry, plumbing, or mechanics; but there are do-it-yourself kits. The contrast of city and country vanishes in endless conurbation. Few children know animals. Even basic foods are packaged and distributed, and increasingly precooked, in the official style.

And a child hears less of any rival style or thought. The rival world-view of (even hypocritical) religion is no longer influential. Children do not know the Bible. Eccentric classical children's literature is discouraged by librarians because it does not fit educators' word-lists and is probably unhygienic. The approved books are concocted according to the official world-view. Other more exciting reading, like comic books, does not contrast to life but withdraws from it, is without reality or feeling. The movies are the same more insidiously, because they are apparently adult and real. Finally, the ideal models of careers with their characters and philosophies—scientist, explorer, nurse, writer—have been normalized to TV stereotypes: they are all the same Organization Man, though they wear various costumes.

## II

Nevertheless, this one system of meaning, although homogeneous and bland, is by no means sparse or quiet. On the contrary, the quantity of public speech, plays, information, cartoons is swamping. The tone is jumpy and distracting. In the schools, exposure occurs with intense pressure of tests for retention and punishment for failure to retain.

No one can critically appreciate so many images and ideas; and there is very little solitude or moratorium to figure them out. A child is confused. And he is also anxious, because if the information is not correctly parroted, he will fall off the school ladder and be a drop-out; or he will not be hep among his little friends.

At a childish level, all this adds up to brainwashing. The components are (a) a uniform world-view, (b) the absence of any viable alternative, (c) confusion about the relevance of one's own experience and feelings, and (d) a chronic anxiety, so that one clings to the one world-view as the only security. This *is* brainwashing.

Of course, in all societies and periods of history small children are subjected to brainwashing, for they are weak, ignorant, economically dependent, and subject to bullying. In some ways in our society the brainwashing of children is not so pernicious as it has been at other times, for there is less corporal punishment, less extreme poverty, less fear of death, and less brutal toilet-training and sexual disciplining. On the other hand, the ideological exposure is unusually swamping, systematic, and thorough. Profit societies, like garrison states, invade every detail of life. But worst of all is that parents are as baffled as the children; since the areas of choice and initiative are so severely limited, they too lose touch with personal and practical information.

Thus, despite our technology of surplus, our civil peace (?), and so much educational and cultural opportunity, it is hard for an American child to grow toward independence, to find his identity, to retain his curiosity and initiative, and to acquire a scientific attitude, scholarly habits, productive enterprise, poetic speech.

## III

Unfortunately, the pervasive philosophy to which children are habituated as they grow up is the orthodoxy of a social machine not interested in persons, except to man and aggrandize itself. Especially not young persons.

Then what happens when, with this background of impersonal and stereotyped language, the child becomes adolescent: awkward and self-conscious, sexually hungry and falling in love, searching for identity, metaphysical, shaken in religious faith or undergoing religious conversion, his Oedipus-complex reviving, making a bid for freedom from home, grandiosely ambitious, looking for a vocation, eager to be serviceable as a human being? At best, in organic communities, rational communication breaks down and the community has recourse to rites of passage.

The American world-view is worse than inadequate; it is irrelevant and uninterested, and adolescents are spiritually abandoned. They are insulated by not being taken seriously. The social machine does not require or desire its youth to find identity or vocation; it is interested only in aptitude. It does not want new initiative, but conformity. Our orthodoxy does not bear metaphysics. Religious troubles are likely to be treated as psychotic; they are certainly disruptive of urban order and scholastic scheduling. Many, maybe most, of the careers that are open are not services to humanity; that is not why businesses are run, nor why bombs are stockpiled. Idealism is astonishingly without prestige.

The adolescent sexual situation is peculiarly ambiguous. We are in a transitional phase of the sexual revolution and there is a breakdown of repression (keeping out of mind) and also less inhibition of sexual behavior. Yet neither in the economy, the housing, nor the family pattern is there any provision for the changed mores. Quite the contrary, the years of tutelage even tend to lengthen, especially for middle class youth in colleges whose administrations regard themselves as *in loco parentis*. The official mental-hygienic ideology bears little relation to the stormy images and imperative demands of adolescent love. In the elementary and junior high schools, sexual facts do not officially exist. But an adolescent is supposed to be sexual or there is alarm.

Embarrassment—the inability to express or reveal one's needs and feelings to the others—is universal among adolescents. But in our society it is especially problematic. The embarrassment contains hostility to those who will not pay attention or will put one down; and also despair at the futility of trying to make oneself clear. For there is not even a common language relevant to one's burning private facts—how pathetic it is to hear adolescents using the language of TV marriage-counsellors, or of movies! Inevitably, silent hostility is retroflected as self-denigration. An adolescent ceases to believe in the rightness of his own wants, and soon he even doubts their existence. His rebellious claims seem even to himself to be groundless, immature, ridiculous.

Broadly speaking, the difficulties of adolescent communication, both in speaking and listening, are kinds of

embarrassment. Let us here discuss adolescent speechless-
ness, in-group language and sub-culture, and how adolescents finally give up their own meaning and swallow
the official adult philosophy hook, line, and sinker.


# IV


Embarrassment may be grounded in too strong desire and confusion, or in hostility and fear.

Paling and blushing embarrassment in expressing lust
or aspiration is largely due to confusion caused by powerful feelings that have been untried, or vague new ideas
that seem presumptuous. It is akin to ingenuous shame,
which is exhibition suddenly inhibited because it is (or
might be) unacceptable. With courage and encourage-
ment, such speechless embarrassment can falter into sweet
or ringing poetic speech, by which the youth explains
himself, also to himself. More common with us, however,
is for the youth to inhibit his stammering and to brazen
out the situation with a line imitated from the mass-media
or salesmanship. For example, the strategy is to "snow"
the girl rather than talk to her. Thereby he proves that
he is grownup, has an erection, etc., but he sacrifices feeling, originality, the possibility of growth, and the possibility of love.

The speechless embarrassment of hostility is fear of
retaliation if one reveals oneself. Suppose a youth is

reprimanded, advised, or perhaps merely accosted by an authoritative adult, e.g. a guidance counsellor; he will maintain a sullen silence and not give the adult the time of day. His presumption is that the adult is setting a trap, could not understand, does not care anyway. The youth cannot adopt a breezy line, as with a peer, for the adult has more words. He will be taken as fresh, hostile, or in bad taste. Therefore it is best to say nothing, expressing (perhaps unconsciously) a blazing contempt. In this situation, the youth's interpretation is not too erroneous, except that the authority is usually not malevolent but busy and perhaps insensitive.

Suppose, however, the adult is a good teacher who does care for the young persons and would like to reach them in meaningful terms, not the orthodoxy. Then, as Frank Pinner has pointed out, it is likely that the teacher's dissenting ideas will be met by a wall of silence that makes communication impossible. The young are so unsure, and their distrust is such, that in the crisis of possible contact they prefer to cling to safe conformity, even though among themselves they may bitterly attack these same conformist ideas.

Even worse, there is an hermetic silence about anything deeply felt or threatening; such things are unspeakable even to one's peers, no less to adults. One may boast to a friend about a sexual conquest or fret about poor grades, but one may not reveal that one is in love or has a lofty aspiration. Or to give a tragic example: Puerto Rican boys will chatter endless small talk and one-up one another, but nobody will mention that one of their number has just been sent to jail or that one has just died of an overdose of heroin. If the forbidden subject is mentioned, they do not hear it. They cannot psychologically afford to relate themselves, their verbal personalities, to the terrible realities of life. (Incidentally, I have heard from teachers in the New York schools that there is a similar cleavage in many young Puerto Ricans' knowledge of the English language. They seem to talk English fluently as long as the subject is superficial and "grown-up"; but they are blank in many elementary words and phrases, and are quite unable to say, in English, anything that they really want or need.)

## V

To diminish embarrassment, since communication with the adults is cut off, there is developed an increasingly exaggerated adolescent "sub-culture," with its jargon, models, authors, and ideology. Let us first distinguish between a "sub-culture" and a "sub-society."

An intense youth sub-society is common in most cultures. In our culture, the interest in sexual exploration, dancing, simple exciting music, athletics, cars and races, clubs and jackets, one-upping conversation, seems to be natural to youth—just as many adult interests are naturally irrelevant and boring to them. Also, the sharing of secrets, often mysterious even to themselves, is everywhere a powerful bond of union among adolescents; and certainly their business is nobody else's business. The Youth Houses of some primitive communities institutionalize all this rather better than our own boarding-schools and colleges, which are too ridden with *in loco parentis* regulations.

The development of such a sub-society into a full-blown sub-culture, however, is not normal, but reactive. It signifies that the adult culture is hostile to adolescent interests, or is not to be trusted; that parents are not people and do not regard their children as people; that the young are excluded from adult activities that might be interesting and, on the other hand, that most adult activities are *not* worth growing up into as one becomes ready for them. Rather, on the contrary, the adults are about to exploit the young, to pressure them into intrinsically boring careers, regardless of proper time or individual choice.

Normally there is not a "youth culture" and an "adult culture," but youth is the period of growing up in the one culture. With us, however, youth feels itself to be almost out-caste, or at least manipulated. It therefore has secrets, jargon, and a lore of sabotage and defense *against* the adult culture.

But then, since the intellectual life of callow boys and girls in isolation from the grown-up economy and culture is thin gruel, youth interests are vastly puffed up into fads, disk-jockeys, politically organized gangs and wars, coterie literature, drugs and liquor, all frantically energized by youthful animal spirits—and cleverly managed by adult promoters. The teen-age market is more than $10 billions a year, in jackets, portable radios, sporting goods, hair-dos, bikes, and additional family cars. Needless to say, this secondary development is simply a drag on the youthful spirit. It is largely frivolous and arbitrary, yet it is desperately conservative and exerts a tremendous pressure of blackmail against non-conformers or those ignorant of the latest, who will be unpopular. It makes it hard to talk sense to them, or for them to talk sense, whether adolescent or adult. And of course there is no chance for intelligent dissent from the official philosophy and standard of life. Naturally, too, especially in the middle class, the regressed adults play at and sponsor every teen-age idiocy.

Inevitably, the high school—with its teen-age majority and adult regime—becomes a prime area for sabotage and other fun and games. I have heard James Coleman, who has most studied these phenomena, express the opinion that the average adolescent is really *in* school, academically, for about ten minutes a day! Not a very efficient enterprise.

A certain number of the young gang up and commit defiant delinquencies. These are partly the revolt of nature—for there is much in our society that is insulting and intolerably frustrating. They are partly reactive against *whatever* happens to constitute "correct" behavior. And they are partly a pathetic bid for attention, as it is said, "We're so bad they give us a Youth Worker."

A pathetic characteristic of recent middle-class

adolescent sub-culture is taking on the language and culture of marginal groups, Negroes and Latin Americans,
addicts, Beat drop-outs from the colleges and the Organized System. This is appropriate, for these others too
are abused and disregarded; they are in the same case as
the adolescents. But such a culture is hardly articulate.
Also there is something exploiting about imitating authentic out-caste people, who live as they do not by
choice but by necessity.

Nevertheless, for many of the woefully embarrassed,
this semi-articulate speech—saying "man" and "cat" and
"like, man"—makes conversation possible. The adolescent
culture is something to talk about and this is a style to
talk in. The words of one syllable of jive, the thoughts
of one syllable of Beat, the content of kicks, movies, and
high school dances, are not a wide discourse, but they
foster being together, and everybody can democratically
participate.

Unfortunately, the small talk drives out real talk.
It is incredibly snobbish and exclusive of sincerity and
originality. Embattled against the adult world that must
inexorably triumph, adolescent society jealously protects
itself against meaning.

## VI

To adolescents of sixteen, the adult world must
seem like a prison door slamming shut. Some must get

jobs which are sure not to fit them and in which they will exercise no initiative whatever. Others must engage in the factitious competition for college-entrance. Either process is formidable with forms and tests. The kids are ignorant of the ropes and ignorant of what they want. Disregarded by the adults, they have in turn excluded adult guidance or ideas looking toward the future. But their adolescent bravado is now seen to be unrealistic and even ridiculous. Having learned nothing, nor fought any battles, they are without morale.

Their weakness can be observed vividly on college campuses. Students gripe about the moral rules by which they are still absurdly harassed at 18 and 19 years of age. It's ironical; if they had quit school and were assembly-line workers, they would be considered responsible enough to come and go, have sex, and drink.—Yet it comes to nothing but griping; they do not feel justified to enforce their demands, for they have never had this issue, or any issue, out with their parents. Similarly, they are unhappy about the overcrowded classes, the credits, the grading; they know they are disappointed in the education they are getting; yet they are so confused about what they do want that they are speechless.

And just in the colleges, which are supposed to be communities of scholars, face-to-face communication is diminished. The adolescent sub-culture that persists is irrelevant to the business going on, except to sabotage it, but the adolescent community is *not* replaced by close acquaintance with learned adults. The teachers hold the students off and, as I argued in *The Community of Schol-*

*ars,* it is a chief function of orderly administration to keep the students out of contact with the teachers and the teachers out of contact with one another. Naturally, as long as the students are isolated with one another, they can be treated as immature, which they are.

The dialogue with the subject-matter, with Nature and History, is as skimpy as with the teacher. Colleges are not interested in such things any more—it has little Ph.D. value. The student is told the current doctrine and is trained to give it back accurately. And, still proving his masculinity and doing a snow-job, the student thinks that the purpose of a course is to "master the subject." Necessarily, in the conflict with the adult world, the young suffer a crushing defeat. There are various ways of surviving it. Some give up on themselves and conform completely—a few indeed become more royalist than the king (but these are often psychopathic, middle-class delinquents). Others make rationalizations: they will return to the fray later when they are "better prepared." Or, "The most important thing is to get married and raise a normal family," they will hold onto feeling and meaning for their family life, or perhaps for their "personal" behavior. A surprising number tell you that the goal of life is $50,000 a year.

The psychology of the introjection is evident: defeated, they identify with what has conquered them, in order to fill the gap with some meaning or other. Once they have made the new identification, they feel strong in it, they defend it by every rationalization.

An alternative philosophy that has recommended

itself to some older adolescents is hipsterism. A hipster cushions the crushing defeat by society by *deliberately* assuming convenient roles in the dominant system, including its underworld, to manipulate it for his own power or at least safety. The bother with this idea—it is the argument of Thrasymachus in Plato's *Republic*—is that the hipster cannot afford to lose himself, or even to become un-selfconscious. He must be ahead of every game. Then he cannot grow by loving or believing anything worthwhile, and he exhausts himself in business with what he holds in contempt, deepening his own cynicism and self-contempt. But hipsterism does provide a satisfaction of mastery and victory which ward off his panic of powerlessness, passivity, and emasculation. It is a philosophy for chronic emergency, during which communication consists inevitiably of camouflage and secrecy, "playing it cool," or of gambits of attack to get the upper hand.

## VII

The conditions that I have been describing, and the youthful responses to them, sadly limit human communication and even the concept of it. "Communication" comes to be interpreted as the transfer of a processed meaning from one head to another which will privately put it in a niche in its own system of meanings. This system is presumably shared with the others—one can never know. And in this presumptive consensus, the exchanged information adds a detail or a specification, but it does not disturb personality or alter characteristic behavior, for the self has not been touched. At most, the information serves as a signal for action from the usual repertory.

Among Americans, this sentiment of consensus, "understanding," is so important that much speech and reading does not even give new information, but is a ritual touching of familiar bases. (This is evident in much newspaper reading, in after-dinner speeches, and so forth.) But the case is not much different with active speech that is supposed to affect choice, e.g. in politics, for no disturbing issues are broached, nor anything that one would have to think new thoughts about. The underlying consensus is assumed—is signalled by the usual words—and no important alternative is offered.

The consensus is *presumably* shared, but any dialectic to test this assumption is in bad form, just as it is impolite to question a loose generalization made in small talk, and say "Prove it." In ideal cybernetic theory, the exchange of information is supposed to alter the organisms conversing, since they must make internal readjustments to it; but my observation is that no such alteration occurs. The chief meaning of conversation is its own smooth going on.

By contrast, the active speech of salesmanship is more lively, because it is meant importantly to change behavior, toward buying something; it is not meant merely to soothe. Thus, strikingly, TV commercials are the only part of TV that makes novel use of the medium itself, employing montage and inventive music, playing with the words, images, and ideas. The pitch of a salesman is likely to be *ad hominem*, in bad form, both flattering and threatening. (Needless to say, there is no dialogue; the hearer is passive or dumbly resistant.) But of course, in salesmanship, apart from the one pre-thought transaction, the consensus is powerfully protected; the TV ad and the program that it sponsors avoid anything that might surprise, provoke, or offend any single person in an audience of millions.

Consider what is lost by this narrow concept of communication as the exchange of processed information with which each communicant copes internally. (a) The function of speech as the shaping expression of pre-verbal needs and experiences, by which a speaker first discovers *what* he is thinking. Such speech cannot be entirely prethought and controlled; it is spontaneous. (b) The function of speech as personally initiating something by launching into an environment that is *unlike* oneself. Initiating, one presumes there is no consensus; otherwise why bother speaking? (c) Most important of all, the function of speech as dialogue between persons *committed to the conversation*—or between a person and a subject-matter in which he is absorbed. This results in change of the persons because of the very act of speaking; they are not fixed roles playing a game with rules.

Speaking is a way of making one's identity, of losing oneself with others in order to grow. It depends not on prior consensus with the others, but on trust of them. But, in my opinion, the speech defined in most contemporary communication theory is very like the speech of the defeated adolescents I have been describing. It is not pragmatic, communal, poetic, or heuristic. Its function is largely to report in a processed *lingua franca*.

Speech cannot be personal and poetic when there is embarrassment of self-revelation, including revelation to oneself, nor when there is animal diffidence and communal suspicion, shame of exhibition and eccentricity, clinging to social norms. Speech cannot be initiating when the chief social institutions are bureaucratized and pre-determine all procedures and decisions, so that in fact individuals have no power anyway that is useful to express. Speech cannot be exploratory and heuristic when pervasive chronic anxiety keeps people from risking losing themselves in temporary confusion and from relying for help precisely *on* communicating, even if the communication is Babel.

As it is, people have to "think" before they speak, rather than risking speaking and finding out what they mean by trying to make sense to others and themselves. In fact, they finally speak English as though they were in school.

# 6

# Programmed

## I

Programmed teaching adapted for machine use goes a further step than conforming students to the consensus which is a principal effect of schooling interlocked with the mass media. In this pedagogic method it is *only* the programmer—the administrative decision-maker—who is to do any "thinking" at all; the students are systematically conditioned to follow the train of the *other's* thoughts. "Learning" means to give some final response that the programmer considers advantageous (to the students). There is no criterion of *knowing* it, of having learned it, of Gestalt-forming or simplification. That is, the student has no active self at all; his self, at least as student, is a construct of the programmer.

What does this imply? Let me analyze a very high-level argument for such teaching by Lauren Resnick, "Programmed Instruction of Complex Skills," in *The Harvard Educational Review* of Fall 1963.

In the conclusion of this perspicuous article, Dr. Resnick tells us:

"By explicit instruction I mean the deliberate modification of the behavior of other human beings. Programmed instruction is not interested in the teacher as stimulator of interest, role model, or evaluator of progress. It is interested in him as instructor, or controller of behavior. This means that programmed instruction is applicable only where we do in fact want to change behavior in a given direction. There are cases where for political or ethical reasons we do not want to. We do not, for example, want to train all students to be active partisans of a given political or religious viewpoint, or make everyone like the same kind of literature or music. In such cases . . . 'exposure' is the most we should attempt." (p. 467)

Let me put this dramatic statement in juxtaposition with an earlier statement in her essay:

"In the context of behavorial analysis, knowledge, skill, and ability can be dealt with only insofar as they can be described in terms of performance. This description is not a matter of listing 'correlates' of ability or knowledge, but of deciding what observable behaviors will be accepted as evidence of their existence. The behaviorist simply eschews the question of whether knowledge, for instance, exists apart from observable behaviors. While, in so doing, he may fail to answer to the philosopher's satisfaction the question, 'What is knowledge?', he very effectively provides himself with a set of usable goals for instruction." (p. 448)

I do not much want to discuss the pedagogic relevance of these ideas. The only evidence of "performance" that school people ever draw on for their experiments is scoring on academic tests, and it seems to be impossible to disabuse school people of the notion that test-passers have necessarily learned anything relevant to their further progress or careers; or of advantage to the body politic; or indeed anything whatever that will not vanish in a short time, when the *real* life-incentive, of passing the test, has passed away. But I want to ask if this kind of *formulation* of teaching does not involve serious legal difficulties, in terms of civil liberties, especially where schooling is compulsory, when the child *must* go to school and submit to having his behavior shaped.

It may seem odd that I keep referring to the constitutional question; but it is a way of asking what kind of democracy we envisage in our curriculum and methods of schooling. Besides, since the young have become so clearly both an exploited and an outcast class, we must begin to think of legal rights.

II

Our Bill of Rights guarantees were grounded in a very different epistemological theory from operant-conditioning, the method that Dr. Resnick has learned from B. F. Skinner. Roughly, the Enlightenment conception was that intellect, like conscience, was something "inward," and the aim of teaching was to nurture its "growth" by "knowledge." Even more important, behavior was the "external" effect of an initiating or self-moving of the "soul"; therefore the student was or became "responsible." In my opinion, the inner-outer metaphor of this conception is quite useless; there is not much use in a psychological theory for entities that are not observable as behavior. But the Aristotelian emphasis on the self-moving organism is solid gold.

Now compulsory schooling, as I have pointed out, was justified in this theory, e.g. by Jefferson, as necessary to bring children to the point of self-government, of exercising citizenly initiative, as well as the animal and social initiative that they had by "nature" and the moral initiative that they had by "conscience." Democracy required an educated electorate. To this was later added the justification that only by compulsory education could the poor get an equal democratic opportunity with the rich; poor parents were likely to put their children to work too early, and not give them a chance to develop to their full powers.

In turn, any course of the curriculum or detail of method was justified by showing that it nurtured the growth of the inward intellect, encouraged initiative, and fitted the young to take a free part in political society. On this view, school teaching was precisely not "training," though parents were allowed to train minor children and the masters of apprentices were allowed to train their bonded apprentices. School subjects either had to contain values ideal in themselves, as good, true, or beautiful, which were "liberal" by definition; or they strengthened the "logical faculty," which the young citizen would then apply to all kinds of matters (this was the traditional notion of "transfer"); or they gave him orientation in space and time—as I have mentioned, especially History was prized, because its horrible and noble examples inspired youth to preserve freedom.

Of course, the late nineteenth century compulsory education in the mechanical arts, to the degree that they were merely utilitarian, could not so easily be justified in these "inward" ways—it tended to seem like apprentice-training at the public expense. But in an expanding economy with high social mobility, and where there was considerable self-employment and much new enterprise, there was no occasion to cavil; a free soul would want such advantageous skills of its own volition. Few adolescents went to school anyway, and children never did have many rights, though plenty of privileges.

## III

Dr. Resnick's system explicitly excludes all notions of "inward" meaning. And she is also unhappy about the sneaking in of any factor of initiative. For example, in discussing Shaping—the approximation of the responses to the final response—she sharply disagrees with those experimenters who wait for the organism to make a small move in the right direction, to reinforce it. "Programmed instruction," she says, "cannot afford to proceed in this way." (But she never does make clear, at least to me, how she gets the beast to move *ab extra*, in order to have something to shape.)

Also, unlike the liberal or "faculty-developing" curriculum of the Enlightenment theory, no particular subject of learning is chosen because of its characteristic appeal to or stimulation of the powers, liberation, or needs of the learner. Operant-conditioning theory, she says, is essentially "contentless"; it is a pure technique that can teach anything to almost anybody. This might be Dr. Conant's "national needs"; it might the the "improved attitudes" of the Continuation branch of Milwaukee Vocational; it might be the vagaries of Big Brother.

In sum, on this view, compulsory schooling, so far as it is programmed, is identical with compulsory training to the goals of the controllers of behavior, and such goals are set by the "we want" of the first paragraph I have cited. Then I am curious to hear from Dr. Resnick the constitutional justification for compulsory schooling in terms of the "we want" and "we do not want" of that paragraph. Who, we? and what limitation is there to "want" or happen to want? The title of her essay, let us remember, is "Instruction of Complex Skills"; she is not restricting behavior-control to rote and drill subjects, but extending it to the higher branches, to criticism, problem-solving, appreciation, except where "we do not want to."

Needless to say, curriculum, methods, and the school-system itself have *always* been determined by social goals and National Goals, parental ambitions, and the need to baby-sit and police the young. But it is one thing to believe—or pretend—that these educate the children, and quite another thing to *say* that they are behavior-controllers.


## IV


Our author's indifference to this kind of consideration appears strongly in an otherwise excellent analysis of the "Discovery Method" as contrasted with step-by-step programmed instruction. One advantage claimed for the Discovery Method—for which, we saw, Dr. Zacharias and the National Science Foundation have manifested enthusiasm—is that the leap over the gap is itself exciting and reinforcing, providing stronger motivation. Dr. Resnick agrees that this might be true for bright students; but she wisely points out that culturally-deprived, poorly achieving youngsters get more satisfaction from steady success, without risk of new failure. A second advantage claimed is that the trial and error in the Discovery process fits the student for the kind of learning that he will have to do outside the classroom; but here Dr. Resnick doubts that the student learns from his errors unless he is trained in what to ask about them, that is, to notice them. (She is right. For example, a good piano teacher will have the student deliberately play the wrong note that he repeats inadvertently.) Finally, it is claimed, the quality of what is learned by Discovery—the synoptic, the law, the solution of the problem—is superior. This, says Dr. Resnick, is because programmed instruction has so far concentrated almost exclusively on teaching mere concepts and information, rather than complex wholes of learning.

What is astonishing in this thoughtful analysis, however, is that she entirely omits the *salient* virtue that most teachers, classical or progressive, have always hoped for in letting the student discover for himself, namely the development of his confidence that he *can*, that he is adequate to the nature of things, can proceed on his own initiative, and ultimately strike out on an unknown path, where there is no program, and assign his own tasks to himself. The classical maxim of teaching is: to bring the student to where he casts off the teacher. Dewey's model for curriculum and method was: any study so pursued that it ends up with the student wanting to find out something further.

Apparently Dr. Resnick cannot even conceive of this virtue, because it is contradictory to the essence of controlled behavior toward a predetermined goal. It is open. From her point of view, it is not instruction at all. In terms of social theory, it posits an open society of independent citizens—but she and Dr. Skinner think there is a special "we" who "want." Also, scientifically, it posits a more open intellectual future than the complex-skill which programming seems to envisage. Is it indeed the case that so much *is* known—so definitely—that we can tightly program methods and fundamental ideas? Much of the program is bound to be out-of-date before the class graduates.

# V

This is a fundamental issue. Intellectually, humanly, and politically, our present universal high-schooling and vastly increasing college-going are a disaster. I will go over the *crude* facts still again! A youngster is compelled for twelve *continuous* years—if middle class, for sixteen years—to work on assigned lessons, during a lively period of life when one hopes he might invent enterprises of his own. Because of the school work, he cannot follow his nose in reading and browsing in the library, or concentrate on a hobby that fires him, or get a job, or carry on a responsible love-affair, or travel, or become involved in political action. The school system as a whole, with its increasingly set curriculum, stricter grading, incredible amounts of testing, is already a vast machine to shape acceptable responses. Programmed instruction closes the windows a little tighter and it rigidifies the present departmentalization and dogma. But worst of all, it tends to nullify the one lively virtue that any school does have, that it is a community of youth and of youth and adults.

Dr. Resnick can assert that there are areas where "we do not want" to control behavior—political, religious, esthetic, perhaps social. But the case is that for sixteen years it is precisely docility to training and boredom that is heavily rewarded with approval, legitimacy, and money; whereas spontaneous initiation is punished by interruption, by being considered irrelevant, by anxiety of failing in the "important" work, and even by humiliation and jail. Yet somehow, after this hectic course of conditioning, young men and women are supposed, on commencement, suddenly to exercise initiative in the most extreme matters: to find jobs for themselves in a competitive market, to make long career plans, to undertake original artistic and scientific projects, to marry and become parents, to vote for public officers. But their behavior has been shaped only too well. Inevitably most of them will go on with the pattern of assigned lessons, as Organization Men or on the assembly-line; they will vote Democratic-Republican and buy right brands.

I am rather miffed at the vulgarity of the implication that, in teaching the humanities, we should at most attempt "exposure"—as if appreciation were entirely a private matter, or a matter of unstructured "emotion." (There is no such thing, by the way, as unstructured emotion.) When Dr. Resnick speaks of the unshaped response to the kind of literature or music "they like," she condemns their esthetic life to being a frill, without meaning for character, valuation, recreation, or how one is in the world. Frankly, as a man of letters I would even prefer literature to be programmed, as in Russia.

That is, *even if behavioral analysis and programmed instruction were the adequate analysis of learning and method of teaching, it would still be questionable, for overriding political reasons, whether they are generally appropriate for the education of free citizens.*

# VI

To be candid, I think operant-conditioning is vastly overrated. It teaches us the not newsy proposition that if an animal is deprived of its natural environment and society, sensorily deprived, made mildly anxious, and restricted to the narrowest possible spontaneous motion, it will emotionally identify with its oppressor and re-spond—with low-grade grace, energy, and intelligence—in the only way allowed to it. The poor beast must do something, just to live on a little. There is no doubt that a beagle can be trained to walk on its hind legs and bal-ance a ball on the tip of its nose. But the dog will show much more intelligence, force, and speedy feedback when chasing a rabbit in the field. It is an odd thought that we can increase the efficiency of learning by nullify-ing *a priori* most of an animal's powers to learn and taking it out of its best field.

It has been a persistent error of behaviorist psychol-ogies to overlook that there are overt criteria that are organically part of *meaningful* acts of an organism in its environment; we can observe grace, ease, force, style, sudden simplification—and some such characteristics are at least roughly measurable. It is not necessary, in describing insight, knowledge, the kind of assimilated learning that Aristotle called "second nature," to have recourse to mental entities. It is not difficult to *see* when a child *knows* how to ride a bicycle; and he never forgets it, which would not be the case if the learning were by conditioning with reinforcement, because that can easily be wiped away by a negative reinforcement. (Kurt Goldstein has gone over this ground demonstratively.)

On the other hand, it is extremely dubious that by controlled conditioning one *can* teach organically meaningful behavior. Rather, the attempt to control *prevents* learning. This is obvious to anyone who has ever tried to teach a child to ride a bicycle; the more you try, the more he falls. The best one can do is to provide him a bicycle, allay his anxiety, tell him to keep going, and *not* to try to balance. I am convinced that the same is true in teaching reading.

## VII

As is common in many (sometimes excellent) modern scientific papers—whether in linguistics or studies of citizen participation or the theory of delinquency—Dr. Resnick asks for more money; and of course, for purposes of pure research, the higher investigations that she asks for should be pursued as long as her enthusiasm lasts and should be supported. Any definite hypothesis that is believed in by a brilliant worker is likely to yield useful by-products that can then be reinterpreted; nor is there any other guide for the advancement of science except the conviction and competence of the researchers.

But I am puzzled at what widespread social benefits she has in mind that warrant a *lot* of expense in brains and machinery. She seems to agree that bright children do not learn most efficiently by these extrinsic methods; and for the average the picture is as I have described it: average employment in a highly automated technology requires a few weeks' training on the job and no schooling at all, and for the kind of humane employment and humane leisure that we hopefully look toward, we require a kind of education and habit entirely different from programmed instruction.

But I am more impressed by what is perhaps Dr. Resnick's deepest concern, the possible *psychotherapeutic* use of more complex programming for the remedial instruction of kids who have developed severe blocks to learning and are far behind. For youngsters who have lost all confidence in themselves, there is a security in being able to take small steps entirely at their own pace and entirely by their own control of the machine. Also, though the chief use of schools is their functioning as a community, under present competitive and stratified conditions it is often less wounding for a kid who has fallen behind to be allowed to withdraw from the group and recover. And this time can usefully and curatively be spent in learning the standard "answers" that can put him in the game again.

There is a pathos in our technological advancement, well exemplified by programmed instruction. A large part of it consists in erroneously reducing the concept of animals and human beings in order to make them machine-operable. The social background in which this occurs, meanwhile, makes many people out-caste and in fact tends to reduce them as persons and make them irresponsible. The refined technique has little valid use for the dominant social group for which it has been devised, e.g. in teaching science; but it does prove to have a use for the reduced out-castes, in teaching remedial arithmetic.

# 7

# Teaching science

A century ago, Matthew Arnold and Thomas Huxley debated whether Science, rapidly growing in importance, should become preponderant over the humanities in the popular curriculum. Arnold opted for the humanities because they give us "criticism of life" and teach us "conduct," the main business of most men. He conceded that for the unusual persons who are scientifically gifted, the philosophy and practice of science itself provide a guide to life. But Huxley's view—in the line leading from the Encyclopedists and Comte to the naturalistic novelists and Veblen—was basically that there is a scientific way of life, a new and better ethic, possible for the majority.

We have seen that the progressive education of the early twentieth century shared this belief in the scientific ethic and added to it the great modern issue: how to be at home in the modern environment which has, willy nilly, become overwhelmingly industrial and technological. In this country, Dewey was a leader in the struggle to secure for science a big place in education. Yet by 1916, Dewey spoke of his "painful" disappointment in the fruits of the scientific curriculum; it had *not* paid off in life-values, but had become scholastic and arid. And we know that in his last period, he estimated more and more highly the experience and structured emotion of art.

By the time we come to C. P. Snow in the fifties, the debate between the humanities and science, like most other serious topics, has become pretty vulgarized. As Snow speaks of them, the humanities are little better than frills and snobbery; but science, correspondingly, is mainly praised as if it were identical with technology and must be universally studied to improve the standard of living of the Africans (though he offers no evidence that, with modern methods of production, we need quite so many technicians to achieve this unexamined purpose). But the nadir of this kind of pitch for science has been, I suppose, the calamitous sentence in the late President Kennedy's message on Education of 1963: "Vast areas of the unknown are daily being explored for economic, military, medical, and other reasons." (The "other reasons" include those of Galileo and Darwin.) Neither the scientific conduct of life, nor any conduct, is thought of as a purpose of education, or thought of at all.

## II

The intervention of the National Science Foundation in improving the science and mathematics courses in the elementary and high schools is on a much higher plane; its avowed aims are reasonable and not base. (It began a few years before the panic about Sputnik, though all the public enthusiasm has been since.) "Literacy in science is becoming essential for all citizens who wish to comprehend the world they live and work in, and to participate in the increasing number of decisions, some of the gravest import, that require an understanding of science. Further, more and more students must be attracted to scientific and technical pursuits, and these students must be prepared to work with increasingly sophisticated ideas and techniques. . . . And there is another aspect . . . more emphasis should be given to disciplined, creative, intellectual activity as an end in itself . . . for each student to experience some of the excitement, beauty, and intellectual satisfaction that scientific pursuit affords." (From the Foreword to *Science Course Improvement Projects*.)

This is a well-rounded educational prospectus, in-

cluding the citizenly, the vocational, and the humanistic.
It is a far cry from "other reasons."

But now another danger has arisen, intrinsic in the
composition of the NSF: the kind of people they consult,
the kind of people they do not consult. Looking at some
of the improved projects and methods reported and the
TV films sponsored, one cannot avoid the impression
that the curriculum-improvers are professors in graduate
schools and cannot finally think of education in science
otherwise than as the producing of Ph.D.'s. "Society,"
says the Foreword a little petulantly, "can no longer
afford to wait a generation or more for new knowledge
to make its way gradually into school and college programs." By Society we may understand M.I.T. etc.

Of course, the Foreword contains the sanitizing dis-
claimer: "Decisions on what to teach remain, in the
healthy American tradition, the exclusive responsibility
of individual schools and teachers. The National Science
Foundation does *not* recommend any specific book, film,
etc. It is hopeful, however, that the products of these
projects will prove to merit serious consideration by
every school and college." This is disingenuous. With the
incredible amounts of national testing, and with actual
courses tailored just for the tests, and with "making the
prestige universities" as the grand goal of all middle-class
parents, college-guidance counsellors, and superintendents of schools, the humble proposals of the NSF have
pretty nearly the force of statutes. . . . The snag is that
there aren't enough competent teachers of the new programs. Bright young graduates in science are more likely

to stay in the universities or go to the corporations than to teach children and adolescents.

(The science-course-improvement studies by the National Service Foundation cost $50 million. When I raised my eyebrows at this sum, a representative of the NSF pointed out to me that this was only 35¢ a person in the United States. "Naw," said a chap from the United Automobile Workers, "it's fifty million dollars.")

What ought science teaching to be about for the great majority who are *not* going to be graduate students in science?

# III

On reflection, there seem to be more than half a dozen plausible reasons for teaching science as a major part of popular education. Let us spell them out and ask their relevance at present:

(1) The pre-training of technicians is not a good reason. The fact that such apprentices must be prepared to work with "increasingly sophisticated ideas and techniques" is rather a reason *not* to emphasize their preparation by general schooling, for obviously the great majority are not going to become such technicians, and the more intense the specialized instruction necessary for some, the less useful for the future of most. Indeed, with the maturing of automation, this objection will be even

stronger: many of the middle technical skills will surely vanish; semi-skilled "technicians" will require *less* pre-training, not more; whereas the high technical skills required will be so far beyond average aptitude that general schools are hardly the place to pre-train them. Like most apprenticeships, this kind can be taught more practically, more specifically, and more quickly by the ultimate employer, without wasting the time of the majority of youngsters on a kind of mathematics and science that they will promptly forget. And it is hard to see why the public should bear the expense for the pre-selection of lively algebrists for General Electric.

(2) On the other hand, the NSF intention of producing original creative scientists seems to me both pretentious and naive. We simply do not know how to breed these, nor whether "schools" are the best place, nor even whether they thrive better by exposure to up-to-date teaching or reaction to out-dated teaching. With a good deal of fanfare, the Woods Hole Conference on science-teaching, on which the NSF relies heavily, arrived at the excellent insights that Dewey had prescribed for teaching any subject whatever: encouraging spontaneity, imagination, courage to guess; avoiding "correct" answers and rejecting all grading and competition; maintaining continuity with emotional and day-to-day experience and having each youngster follow his own path. But are the Woods Hole scientists serious about these insights? I have not heard either Dr. Bruner or the NSF lambasting the achievement tests and the National Merit examination; and what plan do they have to make genuine progressive

education acceptable in the school systems where it is now *less* acceptable year by year?

Even more important, Dewey would never have claimed that these methods have anything to do with high creative invention, any more than finger-painting and teaching art on sound psychological principles will produce masters. Studying the "sources and conditions that stimulate creativity," the late Harold Rugg came to ideas like "preparatory period of baffled struggle," "interlude in which the scientist apparently gives up, pushes the problem 'out of mind' and leaves it for the non-conscious to work upon," "blinding and unexpected flash of insight." Does the NSF have a clear and distinct idea of such processes in the school-system? We have seen that Dr. Zacharias' cautious reliance on the Discovery Method is not for keeps; it is pre-structured to the already known answers of the Ph.D. If the kind of bafflement and resignation necessary for creativity were seriously meant, the appropriate response of a youngster to such hoaxing would be not insight but disgust or rage, as in Zen teaching.

(3) The NSF intention to teach science for its own "excitement, beauty, and intellectual satisfaction" is entirely acceptable; this is science as one of the humanities. The intention is reinforced by the Woods Hole prescription to teach the "fundamental ideas and methods" rather than the current theories which may soon be outmoded anyway. (A sample list of fundamental concepts is Interaction, Physical System, Relativity of Motion, Equilibrium, Energy, Force, Entropy, Organic Evolution.)

Yet once we push these fundamental concepts beyond the stage of philosophical discussion, there arises a dilemma in the nature of the present state of science. It used to be that the chief excitement of science, which is the exploration and discovery of the nature of things, was easy to keep in the foreground; systematic theory was not too far from observation and experiment. Now, however, observation and experiment occur in a vast framework of systematic explanation, and (I would guess) it must be hard to convey the excitement of discovering the truth without what almost amounts to a specialist training. To get to this excitement of actual exploration requires spelling out the fundamental concepts very far; yet without this excitement, the unique contribution of science to the humanities is lost.

Thus, it might still be best, in order to convey to the majority the wonders of exploring and explaining nature, to have recourse to the history of classical experiments, as at St. John's of Annapolis—on the theory that these demonstrate the scientific spirit of man in action; or to stick to the spectacular popular demonstrations that Helmholtz or Huxley used to go in for; or perhaps just to explore the solar system with a 6-inch telescope, plate spoons with silver, cut up dead cats, plant hybrid squash, or time the traffic lights and count the cars, in order to show children and adolescents that there *is* an observable world that can be made intelligible by explanations (what Plato in the *Timaeus* calls "likely stories.")

(4) An even stronger reason for teaching science, which the NSF does not talk about, is its austere moral-

ity, accuracy, scrupulous respect for what occurs. (I myself never learned this and have always regretted it.)
This, I think, is the heart of what Huxley, Veblen, and
Dewey meant by the scientific ethic. But for the majority, unfortunately, this virtue is almost incompatible with
picking up much "content," or in preparing to become a
graduate-student. Simply, the average youngster's chemistry experiment usually does *not* balance out; and moral
science-teaching would then have him spend the entire
semester in explaining the "failure" and cleaning his test-
tubes better. We all know how the student's drawing of
what is seen through the microscope looks remarkably
like the picture in the text-book; this is necessarily
blinked at by the instructor who wants to proceed and
get to the "subject," but of course to condone it destroys
science. The defect is glaringly exaggerated in the TV
lessons, which not only occur as a sleight-of-hand by
experts, but—in every show I have seen—occur entirely
too fast and cover too much ground. Undoubtedly the
live instructor is supposed to retrace the path more thoroughly, but for the average youngster the effect must be
to acquire a system of ideas and explanations, rather than
science. The best students who continue in science will
eventually learn, as real apprentices, the scientific attitude that has been by-passed; yet even graduate students,
like medical students, are often mainly interested merely
in going through the paces and adding to the "system of
science," with appropriate status and rewards.

(5) The NSF purpose "to comprehend the world
one lives and works in" is excellent. But for this purpose,

I wonder whether the NSF projects are not too fancy. The underlying fact is that the average person uses ever more, and more complicated, scientific appliances, yet fewer and fewer of us practically understand or can repair the pump, the electric motor, the automobile that we use. Inevitably, people become slaves to repairmen, and as purchasers and consumers our ignorance is colossal. Correspondingly, the design of scientific appliances is increasingly less transparent, and the manufacturers take no account of their comprehensibility and repairability except by experts. Nor have I heard that industrialists make efforts to instruct their workmen in the overall rationale of the jobs they work at; nor that the labor unions demand it. When the NSF speaks of the need to comprehend in order to overcome the dangerous alienation of modern urban people and workmen, they ought to mean something akin to what progressive educators called "learning by doing"; philosophic concepts and their structuring are *not* sufficient.

(6) The purpose "to participate in grave political decisions on scientific matters" is also extremely valid. If I do not mistake the tone, it is seriously meant by the gentlemen in the NSF, who appreciate the necessity and the dilemma. Decisions involving billions of dollars not only for incomprehensible hardware but in sponsoring research where only a band of experts can even guess the value, and also how to detect phony cover-ups from honorable failures—all these pose an absolutely new problem for democracies. The hope is that by overcoming superstition, including the superstition of "science," by making

people more technically at home, and by teaching the relevant economics and sociology of science-expenditures and scientific castes, the dilemma can be alleviated. (I do not see how it can be solved.) Perhaps we can learn to ask the right questions and judge the authenticity, if not the content, of the answers. And at least on some issues like transportation-policy or the export of technologies in foreign aid, intelligent people would be able to decide better if they dared to criticize the experts at all.

(7) Finally, there is a kind of active participation, more and more incumbent on citizens, that requires a new scientific understanding and judgment. These are the matters of ecology, urbanism, and mental health, where physical, biological, and social sciences interact, that so directly determine everybody's everyday life that we simply cannot afford to leave them to experts. This kind of inquiry—in the line of Patrick Geddes, Lewis Mumford, the decentralists and regionalists—is of course partly political and aesthetic; it over-rides the distinction that we began with, between the sciences and the humanities.

# IV

The kind of science teaching that emerges from this critique of the improved curricula does not fit easily into the up-the-ladder academic system culminating in graduate-schools and the production of Ph.D.'s. A good deal of training is best done in real apprenticeships; learning to be at home with our technology is best done in workshops, and even requires the cooperation of designers and manufacturers; the humanity of science is perhaps best taught to somewhat older students, 18 to 21, and it looks like an excellent subject for Folk Schools like those in Denmark; ecology and urbanism are surely best learned actively in the field, as in the remarkable work of Karl Linn among the underprivileged adolescents of Philadelphia.

Thus we again come to the same conclusion. We ought to spend more of our wealth on education; perhaps especially we need more understanding and practice of science; but it does not follow that the present system of schools is the appropriate institution for the job.

# Part three

# *College*

# 8

# "I don't want to work— why should I?"

## I

At 17 and 18, nearly half go off to something called college, and the others go to work, if there are jobs. We shall see that college is not a very educative environment, but by and large the world of work is even less so.

For most poor urban youth, the strongest present reason to go to work is family pressure; to bring in some money and not be a drag on the hard-working parents who are supporting them. Needless to say, such a reason springs from a complex of problematic emotions: resentment, spite, need for dependency and independence; and from conditions of poverty often at a crisis just at this juncture. As an incentive for finding a job, finding the

right job, or preparing oneself for a job, these are unhappy auspices, and they often operate in reverse, toward
balkiness and truancy.

But the more objective social form of this reason—
"You ought to pull your oar as a member of society; by
the sweat of thy brow shalt thou eat bread"—is nowadays much less telling. We do not have, in America, an
economy of scarcity, only an enormous number of poor
people. To expand the economy still further might well
be politically expedient, to diminish unemployment and
keep up the rate of profit, but the facts are pretty plain
that there is a synthetic demand and an absurd standard
of living. Every kid jeers at the ads. And the prestigious
flashy desirable goods are not such as poor youth beginning in jobs are going to get. In poor neighborhoods the
men who do get them—on credit—are not usually models
for modest labor.

Nor do the idle actually starve. For political and
humanitarian reasons the affluent society doles out a subsistence, although stingy in this as in other public goods
such as education, neighborhood beauty, and care for the
delinquent and insane. And we can hardly expect a youth
to have a sense of responsibility to his community when
every force in modern urban life tends to destroy community sentiment and community functioning.

Perhaps most important of all is that the moral ideology and the dominant economic behavior are entirely
inconsistent. Managers adopt as many labor-saving machines as possible, but the saving of labor is *not* passed
on to society as a whole in shorter work hours, or even

cheaper prices. And even in service-operations where there is no automation, such as restaurants, there is a cutback of employment: bigger crowds, and fewer people to serve them. Yet there is political excitement about unemployment.

Add, finally, that at least 25% of the gross national product is rather directly devoted to the 1,000 overkill.

It is hard to know how much these philosophical considerations weigh with simple folk and children. In a profound sense, people are not fools, and they sniff the atmosphere correctly. In any case, the argument, "If you work, you can hold your head up with self-respect" does not have the overpowering force among our poor youth that it once did. Hipster notions of finding a racket seem also to satisfy the community ethic. And there is even the ethic that to work for a mere living is to be a fool.

## II

There is an evident and sickening disproportion between the money that people work hard for, whether as dish-washer, hospital orderly, stenographer, schoolteacher, or artist, and the "soft" money that comes from expense accounts, tax-dodge foundations, having "made it" as a personality. I have referred to the disproportionate cut of the pie that falls to the academic monks in any welfare operation. Then why should those who are not going to be in the Establishment *work* for money, rather than look for an angle or wait for luck? And it does not help when kids see an immense part of their parents' hard-earned money go on usurious installment payments for high-priced hardware, and rent swallowing up more than a quarter of income.

My guess is that many poor kids are in the cruel dilemma of feeling guilty about not working, and yet uneasy among their peers and even in their own better judgment if they do try to get jobs—especially when trying to get a job has its own degrading humiliations, of confronting prejudice, bureaucratic callousness, and gouging agencies, and often when the young are frustrated by sheer ignorance of how to look for a job at all.

## III

And there is another philosophical aspect, usually overlooked, that is obviously important for these young. I have mentioned it before. So far as they can see—and they see clearly—the absorbing satisfactions of life do *not* require all this work and rat-race. In societies where it is possible to be decently poor, persons of superior education and talent often choose to be poor rather than hustle for money.

In the inflationary American economy, however, decent poverty is almost impossible. To be secure at all, one has to engage in the competition and try to rise; and the so-called "education" is geared to economic advancement. Thus, a common-sensible youth—and especially a poor one whose opportunities for advancement are limited and whose cultural background is unacademic—might reasonably judge that games, sex, and the gang are *preferable* to school and work, but he will then get not independence but misery. He will be so out of things that he will have nothing to occupy his mind. He is disqualified for marriage. He is inferior, out-caste.

As it is, the only ones who can afford the absorbing and simple satisfactions that do not cost much money are those who have succeeded economically and are by then likely unfit to enjoy anything. From this point of view, the chief blessing that our copious society could bestow on us would be a kind of subsistence work that allowed spirited people to be decently poor without frantic insecurity and long drudgery.

## IV

If we turn to the deeper human and religious answers to the question "Why should I work?"—for example, work as fulfillment of one's potentialities, work as the vocation that gives justification—our present economy has little to offer to poor youth.

Unskilled and semi-skilled jobs are parts of elaborate

enterprises rationalized for their own operation and not to fulfill the lives of workmen. Work processes are rarely interesting. Workmen are not taught the rationale of the whole. The products are often humanly pretty worthless, so there is no pride of achievement or utility. Craft and style are built into the machines, lost to the workmen. Labor unions have improved the conditions and dignity of the job, but they have also become bureaucratized and do not give the sense of solidarity.

It is only in the higher job brackets, beyond most poor youth, that there begins to be a place for inventiveness and art; and independent initiative belongs only to top management and expert advisors. There are fewer small shops. Neighborhood stores give way to centralized supermarkets where the employees have no say. There is a great increase in social services, but these require official licenses and are not open to those otherwise qualified who wish to work in them.

The total background of poor youth, including the inadequacies of the schools, conduces to dropping out; but the simplest worthwhile jobs require diplomas.

Here again, it may be asked if these considerations, of vocation, job-interest, job-worthiness, weigh with poor youth. They weigh with everybody. Indeed, the hard task of a youth worker is to find some objective activity that a youth might be interested in, and proud of achieving, that will save him from recessive narcissism and reactive hostility or withdrawal, and give him something to grow on. Further, as I argued in *Growing Up Absurd*, the high premium that workmen put on "Security" is largely a substitute for the feeling of being needed, fully used, indispensable.

## V

Some of the human deficiencies in the jobs can be ameliorated—at least until automation makes the whole matter nugatory by vanishing the jobs. For example, with elementary thoughtfulness, a big plant that has many positions can allow a prospective employee to visit and try out various stations, rather than making an arbitrary assignment. Work processes can be efficiently designed on psychological grounds; for instance, a small group assembling a big lathe from beginning to end, so they have something to show for their day, as the crane carries the product away. In a form of "collective contract" or gang-system used in Coventry, England, fifty workers contract with the firm on a piece-work basis, and then settle among themselves the particular assignments, personnel, schedule, and many of the processes; there must be many industries where this humanizing procedure is feasible. With technical education paid for by industry in cooperation with the schools, we could have more understanding workmen.

The important point is that job-worthiness, the educative value of the job, must be recognized by managers and labor-unions as a specific good.

But of course this is part of the much larger need, to make our whole environment more educative, rather than rigidly restricting the concept of education to what happens in schools.

Socially useful work is probably an indispensable element in the education of most adolescents. It provides an objective structure, a bridge of norms and values, in the transition from being in the family to being oneself. This is the rationale of a good Youth Work Camp, as I described it in *Utopian Essays;* a community of youth democratically directing itself, and controlling itself, to do a job. Many colleges have adopted the Antioch plan of alternating academic periods with periods of work in the economy, which are then made the subject of further academic criticism. But what a pity that precisely the poor youth, who *have* to go to work, get no value from the jobs they work at!

Finally, let me say a word about the miserable job induction at present. I have already mentioned the degrading and humiliating conditions that accompany looking for scarce jobs. Again, we do not appreciate the terrors and hang-ups for the semi-literate and socially paranoiac in filling out personnel forms. Often young human beings are tormented and talent is lost simply for the convenience of business machines. And naturally, for those disposed to feel rejected and inferior, each further frustration rapidly accumulates into an impassable block. A lad soon turns in the form not filled out, or even turns back outside the door. Or, pathetically, there is manic excitement at landing a job which he soon quits or cannot do anyway. The entire process is hopelessly and irrelevantly charged with emotion. And the pitiful and anxious lies that are written on those forms!

Certainly the current proposals to make the school the employment agency are reasonable; the school is at least familiar, even if the kid hates it and has dropped out.

Our classical ideology is that the job should be looked for with resolution and ambition. But how are these possible on the basis of ignorance and alienation? Here as elsewhere, our problem is lapse of community. Our society has less and less community between its adults and its youth. Traditional and family crafts and trades no longer exist, and a youth has few chances to form himself on model workmen in his neighborhood and learn the ropes and opportunities. The difficulties of getting into a union seem, and often are, insuperable. Middle class academic youth in their colleges have at least some contact with the adults who belong to the ultimate job-world, and placement is pretty good. But poor urban youth in schools whose culture is quite alien to them and whose aims fit neither their desires nor their capacities, are among jailers, not models.

These remarks are not optimistic toward solving the problems of employment, and unemployment, of youth. By and large, I think those problems are insoluble, and *should* be insoluble, until our affluent society becomes worthier to work in, more honorable in its functions, and more careful of its human resources.

# 9

# An unteachable
# generation

I

But this is also a hard generation to teach in colleges
what I think ought to be taught. I do not mean that
the students are disrespectful, or especially lazy, or
anything like that; in my experience, they pay us more
respect than we usually deserve and they work as
earnestly as could be expected trying to learn too much
on too heavy schedules. Of course, as I have been
arguing, many of the students, probably the majority,
ought not to be in a scholastic setting at all, and their
presence causes dilution and stupefying standardization
as well as overcrowding. But let us here concentrate on
several other difficulties that are in the very essence of

present-day higher education. (a) The culture we want
to pass on is no longer a culture for these young; the
thread of it has snapped. (b) These young are not
serious with themselves; this is a property of the kind
of culture they do have. (c) And as with the lower
schools, the auspices, method and aims of the colleges
themselves are not relevant to good education for our
unprecedented present and foreseeable future.

## II

The culture I want to teach—I am myself trapped
in it and cannot think or strive apart from it—is our
Western tradition: the values of Greece, the Bible,
Christianity, Chivalry, the Free Cities of the twelfth
century, the Renaissance, the heroic age of Science, the
Enlightenment, the French Revolution, early nineteenth
century Utilitarianism, late nineteenth century Naturalism.

To indicate what I mean, let me mention a typical
proposition about each of these. The Greeks sometimes
aspire to a civic excellence in which mere individual
success would be shameful. The Bible teaches that there
is a created world and history in which we move as
creatures. Christians have a spirit of crazy commitment
because we are always in the last times. Chivalry is
personal honor and loyalty, in love or war. Free Cities

have invented social corporations with juridical rights. The Renaissance affirms the imperious right of gifted individuals to immortality. Scientists carry on a disinterested dialogue with nature, regardless of dogma or consequence. The Enlightenment has decided that there is a common sensibility of mankind. The Revolution has made equality and fraternity necessary for liberty. Utilitarian economy is for tangible satisfactions, not busy-work, money, or power. Naturalism urges us to an honest ethics, intrinsic in animal and social conditions.

Needless to say, these familiar propositions are often in practical and theoretical contradiction with one another; but that conflict too is part of the Western tradition. And certainly they are only ideals—they never did exist on land or sea—but they are the inventions of the holy spirit and the human spirit that constitute the University, which is also an ideal.

Naturally, as a teacher I rarely mention such things; I take them for granted as assumed by everybody. But I am rudely disillusioned when I find that both the students and my younger colleagues take quite different things for granted.

For instance, I have heard that the excellence of Socrates was a snobbish luxury that students nowadays cannot afford. The world "communicated" in the mass media is, effectually, the only world there is. Personal loyalty leaves off with juvenile gangs. Law is power. Fame is prestige and sales. Science is mastering nature. There is no such thing as humanity, only patterns of culture. Education and ethics are what we program for

139

conditioning reflexes. The purpose of political economy is to increase the Gross National Product.

These are not foolish propositions, though I state them somewhat sarcastically. They make a lot of theoretical sense and they are realistic. It is far better to believe them than hypocritically to assert ancient clichés. The bother with these views, however, is that they do not structure enough life or a worthwhile life; that is, as ideals they are false. Or, if they do not pretend to be ideals, what will one do for ideals?

I think that this lack of structure is felt by most of the students and it is explicitly mentioned by many young teachers. They regard me, nostalgically, as not really out of my mind but just out of time and space—indeed, I am even envied, because, although the traditional values are delusions, they do smugly justify, if one believes them and tries to act them. The current views do not mean to justify, and it is grim to live without justification.

There is not much mystery about how the thread of relevance snapped. History has been too disillusioning. Consider just the recent decades, overlooking hundreds of years of hypocrisy. During the first World War, Western culture already disgraced itself irremediably (read Freud's profound expression of dismay). The Russian revolution soon lost its utopian élan, and the Moscow Trials of the thirties were a terrible blow to many of the best youth. The Spanish Civil War was perhaps the watershed—one can almost say that Western culture became irrelevant in the year 1938. Gas chambers and atom bombs showed what we were now capable of, yes our scientists. The Progress of the standard of living has sunk into affluence, and nobody praises the "American Way of Life." Scholars have become personnel in the Organization. Rural life has crowded into urban sprawl without community or the culture of cities. And the Cold War, deterrence of mutual overkill, is normal politics.

In this context, it *is* hard to talk with a straight face about identity, creation, Jeffersonian democracy, or the humanities.

But of course, people cannot merely be regimented; and we see that they find out their own pathetic, amiable, or desperate ideals. Creatureliness survives as the effort to make a "normal" adjustment and marriage, with plenty of hypochondria. The spirit of apocalypse is sought in hallucinogenic drugs. There is para-legal fighting for social justice, but it is hardly thought of as politics and "justice" is not mentioned. On the other hand, some poor youth seem to have quite returned to the state of nature. Art regains a certain purity by restricting itself to art-action. Pragmatic utility somehow gets confused with doing engineering. Personal integrity is reaffirmed by "existential commitment," usually without rhyme or reason.

Unfortunately, none of this, nor all of it together, adds up.

I can put my difficulty as a teacher as follows: It is impossible to convey that Milton and Keats were for real, that they were about something, that they expected that what they had to say and the way in which they said it made a difference. The students can (not brilliantly) tell you about the symbolic structure or even something about the historical context, though history is not much cultivated; but, if one goes back more than thirty years, they don't have any inkling that these poets were writers and *in* a world. And, not surprisingly, young people don't have ancient model heroes any more.

## III

Since there are few self-justifying ideas for them to grow up on, young people do not gain much confidence in themselves or take themselves as counting. On the other hand, they substitute by having astonishing private conceits, which many of them take seriously indeed.

The adults actively discourage earnestness. As James Coleman of Johns Hopkins has pointed out, the "serious" activity of youth is going to school and getting at least passing grades; all the rest—music, driving, 10 billions annually of teen-age commodities, dating, friendships, own reading, hobbies, need for one's own money— all this is treated by the adults as frivolous. The quality or meaning of it makes little difference; but a society is in a desperate way when its music makes little difference. In fact, of course, these frivolous things are where normally a child would explore his feelings and find his identity and vocation, learn to be responsible; nevertheless, if any of them threatens to interfere with the serious business—a hobby that interferes with homework, or dating that makes a youth want to quit school and get a job—it is unhesitatingly interrupted, sometimes with threats and sanctions.

At least in the middle class, that fills the colleges, this technique of socializing is unerring, and the result is a generation not notable for self-confidence, determination, initiative, or ingenuous idealism. It is a result unique in history: *an élite that has imposed on itself a morale fit for slaves.*

The literature favored by youth expresses, as it should, the true situation. (It is really the last straw when the adults, who have created the situation for the young, then try to censor their literature out of existence.) There are various moments of the hang-up. Some stories simply "make the scene," where making the scene means touring some social environment in such a way that nothing happens that adds up, accompanied by friends who do not make any difference. Such stories do not dwell on the tragic part, what is *missed* by making the scene. Alternatively, there are picaresque adventure-stories, where the hipster heroes exploit the institutions of society which are not their institutions, and they win private triumphs. More probingly, there are novels of sensibility, describing the early disillusionment with a powerful world that does not suit and to which one cannot belong, and the subsequent suffering or wry and plaintive adjustment. Or alternatively, the phony world is provisionally accepted as the only reality, and the whole apocalyptically explodes. Finally, there is the more independent Beat poetry of deliberate withdrawal from the unsatisfactory state of things, and making up a new world out of one's own guts, with the help of Japanese sages, hallucinogens, and introspective physiology. This genre, when genuine, does create a threadbare community—but it suits very few.

In order to have something of their own in a situation that has rendered them powerless and irresponsible, many young folk maintain through thick and thin a fixed self-concept, as if living out autobiographies of a life that has been already run. They nourish the conceit on the heroes of their literature, and they defend it with pride or self-reproach. (It comes to the same thing whether one says, "I'm the greatest" or "I'm the greatest goof-off.") They absorbedly meditate this biography and, if vocal, boringly retell it. In this action, as I have said, they are earnest indeed, but it is an action that prevents becoming aware of anything else or anybody else.

It is not an attitude with which to learn an objective subject-matter in college.

## IV

It is also a poor attitude for loving or any satisfactory sexual behavior. Let me devote a paragraph to this.

In my opinion, the virulence of the sexual problems of teen-agers is largely caused by the very technique of socialization, and the irresponsibility consequent on it. (Of course this is not a new thing.) If the young could entirely regulate themselves according to their own intuitions and impulses, there would be far more realism and responsibility: consideration for the other, responsibility for social consequences, and sincerity and courage with respect to own feelings. For example, normally, a major part of attractiveness between two people is fitness of character—sweetness, strength, candor, attentiveness—and this tends to security and realism. We find instead that young people choose in conformity to movie-images, or to rouse the envy of peers, or because of fantasies of brutality or even mental unbalance. In courting, they lie to one another, instead of expressing their need; they conceal embarrassment instead of displaying it, and so prevent feeling from deepening. Normally, mutual sexual enjoyment would lead to mutual liking, closer knowledge, caring for; as St. Thomas says, the chief human end of sexual contact is to get to know the other. Instead, sexual activity is used as a means of conquest and epic boasting, or of being popular in a crowd; and one wants to be "understood" before making love. Soon, if only in sheer self-protection, it is necessary *not* to care for or become emotionally involved. Even worse, in making love, young people do not follow *actual* desire, which tends to have fine organic discrimination and organic prudence; rather, they do what they think they ought to desire, or they act for kicks or for experiment. Normally, pleasure is a good, though not infallible, index that an activity is healthy for the organism; but what one *thinks* will give pleasure is no index at all. There is fantastic excessive expectation, and pretty inevitable disappointment or even disgust. That is, much of the sexual behavior is not sexual at all, but conformity to gang behavior because one has no identity; or proving because one has no other proofs; or looking for apocalyptic experience to pierce the dull feeling of powerlessness.

The confusion is not helped by the adult hypocrisy that says, "Sex is beautiful, a divine creation—for later." It is a pretty makeshift creation that has such poor timing. Is it rather not the duty of society to make its schedule more livable? Consider the following: A psychiatrist in charge of Guidance at a very great university gave a melancholy account of the tragedy of unmarried pregnancy among co-eds. A co-ed asked him why, then, the Infirmary did not provide contraceptives on request. But he refused to answer her question.

V

Still, the chief obstacle to college teaching does not reside in the break with tradition nor in the lack of confidence and earnestness of the students, but in the methods and aims of the colleges themselves. Let me devote the remainder of this little book to this.

# 10

# Two simple proposals

## I

Jacques Barzun, the Dean of Faculties at Columbia, has predicted for us the end of the liberal arts college; it cannot survive the emphasis on technical and professional education and the overwhelming financing of scientific research by Federal money, corporation money, and most of the foundation money.

I think his prediction is justified—I am not so sure I am gloomy about it; if there is a revival of real education in this country, its form and auspices will not look like what we have been used to. But I do not think that the Dean thoroughly understands the causes, or the extent, of the débâcle. For the same social trend, of vocational training and contracted research, spells the end not only of the colleges but of the Universities as well, regarded as schools for independent professionals, communities of scholars, and centers of free inquiry. The crucial issue is not the change from "general" education to "specialism"; and there is nothing amiss in the Sciences having a turn as the preponderant center of studies, since that is the nature of the environment. The medieval universities were mainly professional schools dominated by a kind of metaphysical science, according to their lights. The crucial issue is the change from the humanism of independent guilds of scholars, whether in the liberal arts *or* the professions, to a system of social-engineering for the national economy and polity. The medieval professions and specialties were structured in an ideal world that allowed for communication, that was international, and in which—in an important sense—the professions were oddly spontaneous and free. Our learning is increasingly departmentalized and prescribed.

Our educational reality can be seen in operation in the present kind of scheduling, testing, and grading; and if Dean Barzun is interested in making a change, he can start right here.

Let me repeat the facts. From early childhood, the young are subjected to a lockstep increasingly tightly geared to the extra-mural demands. There is little attention to individual pace, rhythm, or choice, and none whatever to the discovery of identity or devotion to intellectual goals. The aptitude and achievement testing and the fierce competition for high grades are a race up the ladder to high-salaried jobs in the businesses of the world, including the schooling business. In this race, time is literally money. Middle class youngsters—or their parents—realistically opt for Advanced Placement and hasten to volunteer for the National Merit examinations. Negro parents want the same for their children, although the children have less tendency to cooperate.

Disappointingly, but not surprisingly, the colleges and universities go along with this spiritual destruction, and indeed devise the tests and the curricula to pass the tests. Thereby they connive at their own spiritual destruction; yet it is not surprising, for that is where the money and the grandeur are. I do not expect for a moment that they will, in the foreseeable future, recall their primary duties: to pass on the tradition of disinterested learning, to provide a critical standard, to educate the free young (*liberi*) to be free citizens and independent professionals.

The question is, *could* the colleges and universities act otherwise, even if they wished to? Of course they could. Most of them are autonomous corporations. Let me here suggest two modest changes, that are feasible almost immediately, that would entail no risk whatever, and yet would immensely improve these academic communities and importantly liberate them in relation to society.

## II

First, suppose that half a dozen of the most prestigious liberal arts colleges—say Amherst, Swarthmore, Connecticut, Weslyan, Carleton, etc.—would announce that, beginning in 1966, they required for admission a two-year period, after high school, spent in some maturing activity. These colleges are at present five times oversubscribed; they would not want for applicants on *any* conditions that they set; and they are explicitly committed to limiting their expansion.

By "maturing activity" could be meant: working for a living, especially if the jobs are gotten without too heavy reliance on connections; community service, such as the Northern Student Movement, volunteer service in hospital or settlement house, domestic Peace Corps; the army—though I am a pacifist and would urge a youngster to keep out of the army; a course of purposeful travel that met required standards; independent enterprise in art, business, or science, away from home, with something to show for the time spent.

The purpose of this proposal is twofold: to get students with enough life-experience to be educable on the college level, especially in the social sciences and humanities; and to break the lockstep of twelve years of doing assigned lessons for grades, so that the student may approach his college studies with some intrinsic motivation, and therefore perhaps assimilate something that might change him. Many teachers remember with nostalgia the maturer students who came under the GI-bill, though to be sure a large number of them were pretty shell-shocked.

A subsidiary advantage of the plan would be to relieve the colleges of the doomed, and hypocritical, effort to serve *in loco parentis* on matters of morality. If young persons have been out working for a living, or have traveled in foreign parts, or have been in the army, a college can assume that they can take care of themselves.

The American tradition of colleges for adolescents made a kind of sense when the curriculum was largely unquestioned classics, history, and mathematics, taught dogmatically in a seminarian atmosphere, and to an élite that thought it had a justified social role. Present college teaching tries to be something different. It emphasizes method, background reading, criticism, and research, and offers a range of choice or prescription quite baffling to most 17-year-olds. In a curious way, the present dominance of mathematics and physical sciences has resulted in the students being even less mature, yet has obscured the true picture of student ineptitude and professorial frustration. It *is* possible to teach mathematics and physics to boys and girls, especially boys. These abstract subjects suit their alert and schematizing minds, the more so if the teaching treats science as the solution of puzzles. But it is not possible to teach sociology, anthropology, world literature to boys and girls, for they have no experience and judgment. When it is done, the message is merely verbal. The harsh facts and the relativity of morals are bound to be embarrassing and shocking. Regarded as "assignments"—as high school graduates must regard them—the voluminous readings are indigestible straw and are annotated by rote; more mature students might be able to take them as books. In brief, whiz-bang youngsters who have found their identity as mathematicians, chemists, or electronic technicians might well speed on to M.I.T. at age 15. The liberal arts colleges, that are essentially concerned with educating citizens and statesmen, social scientists and social professionals, scholars and men-of-letters, require more maturity to begin with. If the average age of entrance were higher, these colleges would also serve as the next step for the many disappointed science-students, who can hardly be expected to backtrack among the seventeens. (A very numerous group switch from the physical sciences to the social sciences and humanities.)

Throughout our educational system there is a desperate need for institutional variety and interims in which a youth can find himself. If we are going to require as much schooling as we do, we must arrange for breaks and return-points, otherwise the schooling inevitably becomes spirit-breaking and regimentation. In my opinion, however, a much more reasonable over-all pattern is to structure all of society and the whole environment as educative, with the schools playing the much more particular and traditional role of giving intensive training when it is needed and sought, or of being havens for those scholarly by disposition.

154

## III

My other proposal is even simpler, and not at all novel. Let half a dozen of the prestigious Universities— Chicago, Stanford, the Ivy League—abolish grading, and use testing only and entirely for pedagogic purposes as teachers see fit.

Anyone who knows the frantic temper of the present schools will understand the transvaluation of values that would be effected by this modest innovation. For most of the students, the competitive grade has come to be the essence. The naive teacher points to the beauty of the subject and the ingenuity of the research; the shrewd student asks if he is responsible for that on the final exam.

Let me at once dispose of an objection whose unanimity is quite fascinating. I think that the great majority of professors agree that grading hinders teaching and creates a bad spirit, going as far as cheating and plagiarizing. I have before me the collection of essays, *Examining in Harvard College*, and this is the consensus. It is uniformly asserted, however, that the grading is inevitable; for how else will the graduate schools, the foundations, the corporations *know* whom to accept, reward, hire? How will the talent scouts know whom to tap?

By testing the applicants, of course, according to the specific task-requirements of the inducting institution, just as applicants for the Civil Service or for licenses in medicine, law, and architecture are tested. Why should

Harvard professors do the testing *for* corporations and graduate-schools?

The objection is ludicrous. Dean Whitla, of the Harvard Office of Tests, points out that the scholastic-aptitude and achievement tests used for *admission* to Harvard are a super-excellent index for all-around Harvard performance, better than high-school grades or particular Harvard course-grades. Presumably, these college-entrance tests are tailored for what Harvard and similar institutions want. By the same logic, would not an employer do far better to apply his own job-aptitude test rather than to rely on the vagaries of Harvard section-men. Indeed, I doubt that many employers bother to look at such grades; they are more likely to be interested merely in the fact of a Harvard diploma, whatever that connotes to them. The grades have most of their weight with the graduate schools—here, as elsewhere, the system runs mainly for its own sake.

It is really necessary to remind our academics of the ancient history of Examination. In the medieval university, the whole point of the gruelling trial of the candidate was whether or not to accept him as a peer. His disputation and lecture for the Master's was just that, a master-piece to enter the guild. It was not to make comparative evaluations. It was not to weed out and select for an extra-mural licensor or employer. It was certainly not to pit one young fellow against another in an ugly competition. My philosophic impression is that the medievals thought they knew what a good job of work was and that we are competitive because we do not know. But the more status is achieved by largely irrelevant competitive evaluation, the less will we ever know.

(Of course, our American examinations never did have this purely guild orientation, just as our faculties have rarely had absolute autonomy; the examining was to satisfy Overseers, Elders, distant Regents—and they as paternal superiors have always doted on giving grades, rather than accepting peers. But I submit that this set-up itself makes it impossible for the student to *become* a master, to *have* grown up, and to commence on his own. He will always be making A or B for some overseer. And in the present atmosphere, he will always be climbing on his friend's neck.)

Perhaps the chief objectors to abolishing grading would be the students and their parents. The parents should be simply disregarded; their anxiety has done enough damage already. For the students, it seems to me that a primary duty of the university is to deprive them of their props, their dependence on extrinsic valuation and motivation, and to force them to confront the difficult enterprise itself and finally lose themselves in it.

*proposal #2 abolish grading*

A miserable effect of grading is to nullify the various uses of testing. Testing, for both student and teacher, is a means of structuring, and also of finding out what is blank or wrong and what has been assimilated and can be taken for granted. Review—including high-pressure review—is a means of bringing together the fragments, so that there are flashes of synoptic insight.

There are several good reasons for testing, and kinds of test. But if the aim is to discover weakness, what is the point of down-grading and punishing it, and thereby inviting the student to conceal his weakness, by faking and bulling, if not cheating? The natural conclusion of synthesis is the insight itself, not a grade for having had it. For the important purpose of placement, if one can establish in the student the belief that one is testing *not* to grade and make invidious comparisons but for his own advantage, the student should normally seek his own level, where he is challenged and yet capable, rather than trying to get by. If the student dares to accept himself as he is, a teacher's grade is a crude instrument compared with a student's self-awareness. But it is rare in our universities that students are encouraged to notice objectively their vast confusion. Unlike Socrates, our teachers rely on power-drives rather than shame and ingenuous idealism.

Many students are lazy, so teachers try to goad or threaten them by grading. In the long run this must do more harm than good. Laziness is a character-defense. It may be a way of avoiding learning, in order to protect the conceit that one is already perfect (deeper, the despair that one *never* can). It may be a way of avoiding just the risk of failing and being down-graded. Sometimes it is a way of politely saying, "I won't." But since it is the authoritarian grown-up demands that have created such attitudes in the first place, why repeat the trauma? There comes a time when we must treat people as adult, laziness and all. It is one thing courageously to fire a do-nothing out of your class; it is quite another thing to evaluate him with a lordly F.

Most important of all, it is often obvious that balking in doing the work, especially among bright young people who get to great universities, means exactly what it says: The work does not suit me, not this subject, or not at this time, or not in this school, or not in school altogether. The student might not be bookish; he might be school-tired; perhaps his development ought now to take another direction. Yet unfortunately, if such a student is intelligent and is not sure of himself, he *can* be bullied into passing, and this obscures everything. My hunch is that I am describing a common situation. What a grim waste of young life and teacherly effort! Such a student will retain nothing of what he has "passed" in. Sometimes he must get mononucleosis to tell his story and be believed.

And ironically, the converse is also probably commonly true. A student flunks and is mechanically weeded out, who is really ready and eager to learn in a scholastic setting, but he has not quite caught on. A good teacher can recognize the situation, but the computer wreaks its will.

# 11

# A usual case—
# nothing fancy

## I

To sum up these dour remarks about American schools in the middle of the twentieth century, consider a usual case. Here is a young fellow in a college classroom. *He* is not usual, for everybody is unique, but his case is usual. His face is pretty blank but he is sitting in a middle row, not, like some, in the rear near the door, ready to bolt. Let me review a dozen important facts about his situation—they are obvious, nothing fancy.

He is in his junior year. So, omitting kindergarten, he has been in an equivalent classroom for nearly fifteen continuous years, intermitted only by summer vacations for play. Schooling has been the serious part of his life, and it has consisted of listening to some grown-up talking and of doing assigned lessons. The young man has almost never seriously assigned himself a task. Sometimes, as a child, he thought he was doing something earnest on his own, but the adults interrupted him and he became discouraged.

He's bright—he can manipulate formulas and remember sentences, and he has made a well-known college. During his last year in high school, he made good grades on a series of gruelling State and National Tests, Regents, College Boards, National Merits, Scholastic Aptitudes. And in this college, which is geared to process Ph.D.'s, he has survived, though the attrition is nearly 40%. He has even gotten a partial scholarship on the National Defense Education Act. Yet, as it happens, he doesn't like books or study at all. He gets no flashes of insight into the structure or the methods of the academic subjects. This isn't the field in which his intelligence, grace, and strength of mind and body show to best advantage. He just learns the answers or figures out the puzzles. Needless to say he has already forgotten most of the answers that he once "knew" well enough to pass, sometimes brilliantly.

The academic subject being taught in this particular classroom is intrinsically interesting; most arts and sciences are intrinsically interesting. The professor and even the section-man know a good deal about it, and it is interesting to watch their minds work. But it is one of the social sciences and our young man does not grasp that it is *about* something; it has no connection for him.

He has had so little experience of society or institutions. He has not practiced a craft, been in business, tried to make a living, been married, had to cope with children. He hasn't voted, served on a jury, been in politics, nor even in a youth movement for civil rights or peace or Goldwater. Coming from a modest middle class suburb, he has never really seen poor people or foreigners. His emotions have been carefully limited by the conventions of his parents and the conformism of his gang. What, for him, could history, sociology, political science, psychology, classical music or literature, possibly be about? (In the *Republic*, Plato forbids teaching most of our academic subjects until the student is thirty years old! Otherwise the lessons will be mere sophistry, emptily combative.)

Our young man is not verbally combative, and he's not a hipster who talks out to show that he knows the score, in order to put you down. But sometimes he is teased by something that the teacher or the book says, and he wants to demur, argue, ask a question. But the class is too crowded for any dialogue. When the format is a lecture, one cannot interrupt. Perhaps the chief obstacle to discussion, however, is the other students. In their judgment, discussion is irrelevant to the finals and the grades, and they resent wasting time. Also, they resent it if a student "hogs attention."

From time to time, the teacher, especially the young section-man, is heartened by a sign of life and does want to pursue the discussion. He is himself given to expressing dissenting opinions, questioning the justification of an institution or asking a student for evidence from personal experience. At once a wall of hostility rises against the teacher as well as the questioning student. Surely he must be a communist, pacifist, or homosexual. Maybe he is ridiculing the class. Feeling the hostility and being a rather timid academic, worried about advancement and ultimate tenure, the teacher signs off: "Well, let's get back to the meat of the course . . . that's beyond our scope here, why don't you take Sosh 403? . . . that's really anthropology, young man, and you'd better ask Professor O'Reilly, heh heh."

Indeed, little of the teaching makes our student see the relevance, necessity, or beauty of the subject. The professor, especially, is interested in the latest findings and in the ingenuity of a new technique, but the student is at sea as to why he is studying it at all, except that it's part of sequence B toward a Bachelor's. The confusion is made worse, as I have said, by the fact that the present young generation, including the young teachers, has at most a tenuous loyalty to the culture of the Western world, the Republic of Letters, the ideal of disinterested Science. But apart from this tradition, the University is nothing but a factory to train apprentices and process academic union-cards.

Yet a college is a poor environment in which to train apprentices, except in lab sciences where one works at real problems with the real apparatus. Most of the academic curriculum, whether in high school or college, is abstract in a bad sense. It must be so. A structure of ideas is abstracted from the on-going professions, civic and

business activities, social institutions; and these ideas are
again thinned out and processed to be imported into classrooms and taught as the curriculum. To be sure, this
ancient procedure often makes sense. It makes sense for
aspiring professionals who know what they are after and
want a briefing; and it makes sense for the scholarly who
have a philosophical interest in essences and their rela-
tionship, and want to chart the whole field. But for most,
the abstractness of the curricular subjects, especially if
the teaching is pedantic, can be utterly barren. The lessons are only exercises, with no relation to the real world.
They are never for keeps. And many of the teachers are
merely academics, not practicing professionals; they are
interested in the words and the methodology, not the
thing and the task.

## II

The young man respects his teachers and he knows
it is a good school, almost a prestige school, but he cannot
help feeling disappointed. He had hoped in a vague way
that when he came to college it would be different from
high school. He would be a kind of junior friend of
learned men who had succeeded; he could model himself on them. After all, except for parents and school-
teachers—and the school-teachers have been prissy—he
has had little contact with any adults in his whole life.

He thought, too, that the atmosphere of learning in college would, somehow, be free, liberating, a kind of wise bull-session that would reveal a secret. But it has proved to be the same cash-accounting of hours, tests, credits, grades. The professor is, evidently, preoccupied with his own research and publishing. In both class and office-hours he is formal and stand-offish. He never appears in the coffee-shop, never invites one home. He certainly never exposes himself as a human being. He is rather meticulous about the assignments being on time and he is a "tough" grader, but this seems to be his way of keeping the students under control, rather than due to belief in the system. He does not seem to realize that they respect him anyway.

So, just as in high school, the youth are driven back on their exclusive "sub-culture," which only distracts further from any meaning that academic life might have. As Riesman and others have pointed out, the students and faculty confront one another like hostile, or at least mutually suspicious, tribes.

Also, this past decade, the lack of community has been vastly exacerbated by the state of chaotic transition in which almost every college in the country exists. The grounds are torn up by bulldozers; the enrollment is excessive; the classes are too large; the students are housed three and four in a room meant for two. The curriculum is continually in process of readjustment. Professors are on the move, following the contracted research, or pirated away by salary hikes. These conditions are supposed to be temporary, but I have seen them now for ten years and the immediate future will be worse. A whole generation is being sacrificed.

An even deadlier aspect of the expansion is the unabashed imperialism of the administrators. This leads to entirely phony operations. Excellent teachers and scholars are scuttled for spectacular names that will never teach. A reputation for innovation and daring is sought, but student publications are censored in order to protect the Image. Scores of millions of new endowments are boasted of, but there is unbelievable penny-pinching about deficits in the cafeteria, rent for the dormitories, tuition, instructors' salaries.

Another aspect of transition is the Knowledge Explosion. New approaches and altogether new subjects must be taught, yet the entrenched faculty are by no means willing to give up any of the old prescribed subjects. It is peculiar; one would expect that, since the professors have tenure, they would welcome dropping some of the course load; but their imperialism is strong too, and they will give up nothing. So our student is taking five or even six subjects, when the maximum should be three. Whenever he begins to be interested in a subject, he is interrupted by other chores. Rushed, he gives token performances, which he has learned to fake. No attention is paid to what suits *him*. The only time a student is treated as a person is when he breaks down and is referred to Guidance.

In place of reliance on intrinsic motives, respect for individuality, leisurely exploration, there is a stepped-up pressure of extrinsic motivations, fear and bribery. The student cannot help worrying about his father's money, the fantastic tuition and other fees that will go down the drain if he flunks out; and he must certainly keep his scholarship. On the other hand, the talent scouts of big corporations hover around with lavish offers. In this atmosphere are supposed to occur disinterested scrutiny of the nature of things, the joy of discovery, moments of creativity, the finding of identity and vocation. It is sickening to watch.

## III

Finally, we must say something about the animal and community life from which our collegian has come into this classroom. The college has spent government and foundation money in pretentious buildings with plushy lounges, but the food is lousy and the new dormitories are like bedlam for want of sound-proofing. The values of college presidents are incredibly petty-bourgeois; their world is made for photographs, not to live in.

The Administration has set itself strongly against fraternity-houses because of the exclusion-clauses and to promote cohesiveness of the community. These are excellent reasons, but one sometimes has a strong suspicion that the reality is to fill the new dormitories, built with Urban Renewal funds. If students want to live off-campus in their own cooperatives, they are avuncularly told that, at 20 years old, they are not mature enough to feed their faces and make their beds.

No attempt is made by the University to come to terms with its neighbors. Rather, to expand, it has the neighborhood condemned as a slum and it dislocates residents of many years. Then it asks for police protection because of the social tension. Some students vanish into the condemnable or condemned neighborhood and the campus sees little of them except for classes. Other students more hospitably invite the neighbors to Saturday night dances, with a local jazz combo, but the Dean breaks it up by having a cop ask for ID cards.

There are exquisitely elaborate regulations for sexual and convivial behavior—days and hours and how many inches the door must be open and whose feet must be on the ground. The Administration claims to be *in loco parentis*, yet half the young men and women had more freedom at home, when they were kids in high school. One has more than a strong suspicion, and not sometimes but usually, that all the parental concern is merely for Public Relations. The college motto is *Lux et Veritas*, but there is a strong smell of hypocrisy in the air.

Maybe the most galling thing of all is that there is a Student Government, with political factions and pompous elections. It is empowered to purchase the class rings and organize the Prom and the boat-ride. Our young man no longer bothers to vote. But when there is a need to censor the student paper or magazine, the Administration appoints these finks to be on a joint faculty-student board of review, so that the students are made responsible for their own muzzling.

## IV

Our junior's face now isn't quite so blank. It is wearing a little smile. The fact is that he is no longer mechanically taking notes but is frankly day-dreaming, as he used to in the sixth grade.

The prospect is appalling. There might be four or five more years of this, since his father wants him to continue in graduate school, and he no longer has any plans of his own anyway. Think of it! He will now be doing "original research" under these conditions of forced labor. And besides, since he will have a wife, a small child, and another on the way, he will be panicky that he might not get the assistantship.

Of course, many of the unfavorable college conditions which I have been describing can, and should, be improved. There are a number of expedients. The grading can be scrapped, keeping the testing as a pedagogic method. There can be many part-time active professionals in the faculty, to generate a less academic atmosphere. There are several arrangements for teachers to pay attention to students, discover their intrinsic motivations, guide them in more individual programs. The social sciences can be made less unreal by working pragmatically on problems of the college community itself and the immediate rural or city environment. The moral rules can be reformed to suit an educational community, teaching responsibility by giving freedom in an atmosphere of counsel and support. So forth and so on.

Nevertheless, when we consider those fifteen years, and sixteen years, and twenty years of schooling, we cannot avoid the disturbing question: Why is the young man in such a classroom altogether? It suits him so badly. He is bright but not bookish, curious but not scholarly, teachable but not in this way.

He must be educated; everybody must be educated; but this kind of schooling has certainly not been the best way to educate him. We have seen him in other situations than school when he looked far brighter, both more spontaneous and more committed; when he showed initiative and was proud of what he was doing; when he learned a lot, fast, simply because he wanted to or had to. Maybe, for him, the entire high school and college institution, in the form that we know it, has been a mistake.

If so, what a waste of his youth and of the social wealth! And it is this waste that we are busy expanding to 50% going to college by 1970.

## V

The argument of this book is that every child must be educated to the fullest extent, brought up to be useful to society and to fulfill his own best powers. In our society, this must be done largely at the public expense, as a community necessity. Certainly the Americans ought to spend more on it than they do, instead of squandering so much on piggish consumption, hardware, and highways. But it is simply a superstition, an official superstition and a mass superstition, that the way to educate the majority of the young is to pen them up in schools during their adolescence and early adulthood.

The hard task of education is to liberate and strengthen a youth's initiative, and at the same time to see to it that he knows what is necessary to cope with the on-going activities and culture of society, so that his initiative can be relevant. It is absurd to think that this task can be accomplished by so much sitting in a box facing front, manipulating symbols at the direction of distant administrators. This is rather a way to regiment and brainwash.

At no other time or place in history have people believed that continuous schooling was the obvious means to prepare most youth for most careers, whether farmer, industrial worker, craftsman, nurse, architect, writer, engineer, lawyer, shopkeeper, party-boss, social worker, sailor, secretary, fine artist, musician, parent, or citizen. Many of these careers require a lot of study. Some of them need academic teaching. But it was never thought useful to give academic teaching in such massive and continuous doses as the only regimen.

The idea of everybody going to a secondary school and college has accompanied a recent stage of highly centralized corporate and state economy and policy. Universal higher schooling is not, as people think, simply a continuation of universal primary schooling in reading and democratic socialization. It begins to orient to careers and it occurs after puberty, and jobs and sex are usually not best learned about in academies. The bother is, however, that the long schooling is not only inept, it is psychologically, politically, and professionally, damaging.

In my opinion, there *is* no single institution, like the monolithic school-system programmed by a few graduate universities and the curriculum reformers of the National Science Foundation, that can prepare everybody for an open future of a great society.

Thus at present, facing a confusing future of automated technology, excessive urbanization, and entirely new patterns of work and leisure, the best educational brains ought to be devoting themselves to devising *various* means of educating and paths of growing up, appropriate to various talents, conditions, and careers. We should be experimenting with different kinds of school, no school at all, the real city as school, farm schools, practical apprenticeships, guided travel, work camps, little theaters and local newspapers, community service. Many others, that other people can think of. Probably more than anything, we need a community, and community spirit, in which many adults who know something, and not only professional teachers, will pay attention to the young.

But the tendency is in just the opposite direction, to concentrate, aggrandize, and streamline what we have. With the unanimous applause of all right-thinking people, Congress (1963) appropriated another two billions for college buildings. The foundations increasingly underwrite scholarships and professional salaries. Of the fifteen billions budgeted in 1962 by the Federal Government for Research and Development, two billions went directly to the Universities and the rest largely underwrote Ph.D.'s and prospective Ph.D.'s. Fifty millions went to the National Science Foundation just for studies in improving primary and high school courses. There is a vigorous campaign by the President to cajole and threaten the drop-outs back into school, and we saw that the Secretary of Labor asked to extend the compulsory age to 18. And all this goes almost entirely unquestioned, even by know-nothing politicians who refuse to spend anything on any other kind of public goods. In plans to pump-prime the economy, even in such a splendid document as the Manifesto on the Triple Revolution, money for Schools is often Number One, or else Number Two, right after Housing. Among all liberals and champions of the underprivileged, it is an article of faith that salvation for the Negroes and Spanish-Americans consists in more schooling of the middle class variety. And further, all philosophers, from hard-liners like Rickover, through James Conant, to free-thinkers like Martin Mayer, insist that salvation for society consists in tightening and up-grading middle class schools, and getting rid of progres-sive education.

Like any mass belief, the superstition that schooling is the only path to success is self-proving. There are now no professions, whether labor-statesman, architect, or trainer in gymnastics, that do not require college diplo-mas. Standards of licensing are set by Boards of Regents that talk only school language. For business or hotel-management it is wise to have a Master's. Across to the billions for Research and Development is by the Ph.D. in physical sciences, and prudent parents push their chil-dren accordingly; only a few are going to get this loot, but all must compete for it. And so we go down to the diplomas and certificates required for sales-girls and typists. If you are Personnel, you need a piece of paper to apply, and almost everybody is Personnel. Thus, ef-fectively, a youth *has* no future if he quits, or falls off, the school ladder. Farm youth can still drop out with-out too much clatter, but the rural population is now 8% and rapidly diminishing.

If, in this climate of opinion, I demur, I am accused of being against the National Goals and against suburbia. So I am. But on the other hand, I have been accused of being a racist-élitist who thinks that some people are "not good enough" to go to school. But I am not an élitist and I do not think that some people are not good enough. The scholastic disposition is a beautiful and useful one; we are lucky that a minority of people are so inclined. But I do not think it is the moon and the stars.

## VI

To understand our present situation, let us review the history of schooling in this century.

By 1900, our present school system was established in its main outlines, including the liberal arts colleges and the German-imitating Universities. At that time there was almost universal primary schooling in a great variety of local arrangements, yet—we saw—only 6% of the 17-year-olds graduated from high school. Maybe another 10% would have graduated if they could have afforded it. (Recently, Dr. Conant has estimated that 15% are academically talented.) We may assume that that 6% or 16% would be in school because they wanted to be there; not only would there be no startling problems of discipline, but they could be taught a curriculum, whether traditional or vocational, that was interesting and valuable for itself. They were not conscripted soldiers, being chased up a ladder.

Now the 94% who did not graduate obviously were not "drop-outs." They were everybody: future farmer, shopkeeper, millionaire, politician, inventor, journalist. Consider the careers of two master architects who were born around that time. One quit school at eighth grade to leave home and support himself. Gravitating to an architect's office as an office-boy, he found the work to his liking. He learned draftsmanship in various offices, and French and mathematics on the outside (with the help of friendly adults), and he eventually won the Beaux

Arts prize and studied in a Paris *atelier*. He has since built scores of distinguished buildings and, as the graduate professor of design at a great university, is one of the most famous teachers in the country. The other architect is the most successful in America in terms of the size and prestige of his commissions. He quit school at age 13 to support his mother. Working for a stone-cutter, he learned to draw, and in a couple of years he cut out for New York and apprenticed himself to an architect. In competition with a room-mate, he studied languages and mathematics. Via the Navy in 1918, he got to Europe with some money in his pocket and traveled and studied. Returning, he made a splendid marriage, and so forth.

These two careers, not untypical except for their *éclat*, are almost unthinkable at present. How would the young men be licensed without college degrees? How would they get college degrees without high school diplomas? But these men had the indispensable advantage that they were deeply self-motivated, went at their own pace, and could succumb to fascination and risk. Would these two have become architects at all if they were continually interrupted by high school Chemistry, Freshman Composition, Psychology 106, at a time when they didn't care about such things? (But they have learned them since, nevertheless!)

It would be a useful study—for a Master's thesis?—to find how many people who grew up from 1900 to 1920 and have made great names in the sciences, arts, literature, government, business, etc. actually went through the *continuous* sixteen-year school grind, without quitting, or without quitting and occasionally returning when it was relevant.

As the decades passed, higher schooling began to be a mass phenomenon. In 1930, 30% graduated from high school and 11% went to college. By 1963, we see that 65% have graduated, of whom more than half go to college.

Who now are the other 35%? They are the Dropouts, mostly urban-underprivileged or rural. From this group we do not much expect splendid careers, in architecture, politics, or literature. They are not allowed to get jobs before 16; they find it hard to get jobs after 16; they might drop out of society altogether, because there is now no other track than going to school.

# VII

What happened to the schools during the tenfold increase from 1900 to 1960? Administratively, we saw, we simply aggrandized and bureaucratized the existing framework. The system now looks like the system then. But in the process of massification, it inevitably suffered a sea-change. Plant, teacher-selection, and methods were increasingly standardized.. The "students" became a different breed. Not many were there because they wanted to be there; a lot of them, including many of the bright and spirited, certainly wanted to be elsewhere and began to make trouble. The academic curriculum was necessarily trivialized. An important function of the schools began to be baby-sitting and policing. The baby-sitting was continued into the rah-rah colleges.

Naturally, in the aggrandized system, Educational Administration became very grand. To say it brutally, this was importantly because of the very irrelevance of the system itself, the inappropriate students and the feeble curriculum. Stuck with a bad idea, the only way of coping with the strains was to have more Assistant Principals, Counsellors, Truant Officers, University Courses in Methods and Custodial Care, Revised Textbooks. Currently we are getting Team Teaching, Visual Aids, Higher Horizons, Programmed Instruction. To compensate for the mass trivializing of the curriculum, there are Intellectually Gifted Classes, Enrichment, and Advanced Placement. And on the other hand, Opportunity Classes for the dull and 600 Schools for the emotionally disturbed. The freshman year in college has been sacrificed to Surveys and Freshman Composition, to make up for lost ground and weed out the unfit.

Correspondingly, from 1910 on, the age of Frederick Taylor, school superintendents have become Scientific Business Managers and Educators with a big E. College Presidents have become mighty public spokesmen. Public Relations flourish apace.

Till recently, however, the expansion was fairly harmless, though plenty foolish. It was energized by a generous warm democracy and an innocent seeking for prestige by parents becoming affluent. These were not new things in America, or elsewhere. By and large, the pace was easy-going. Children were not fed tranquillizers; few adolescents had cause to suffer nervous breakdowns because of the testing; and collegians could get a gentlemanly C by coasting.

The unfortunate part of the expansion was that, insensibly, everybody began to believe that being in school was the only way to become an educated person. What a generation before had been the usual course, to quit school and seek elsewhere to grow up, became a sign of eccentricity, failure, delinquency.

## VIII

Suddenly, since the Korean war and hysterically since Sputnik, there has developed a disastrous overestimation of schools and scholarship. More basically, there has been a dramatic shift in economic power—climaxing in the Kennedy regime—toward electronic and other high-technological industries, and the ascendancy of the National Science Foundation and the Universities both in and outside of government. Also, since the end of World War II, the income-spread between the haves and have-nots has steadily increased; there is immense new production of wealth, but in the structure of the economy, it does not filter down.

So we see that mothers who used to want their offspring to be "well adjusted," are now mad for the I.Q. and the Percentile. Schools that were lax, democratic or playful, are fiercely competitive. And an average un-bookish youth finds himself in a bad fix. He may not be able to cope with the speed-up and the strict grading, yet if he fails there are loud alarms about his pre-delin-quency, and there are national conferences on drop-outs.

We are witnessing an educational calamity. Every kind of youth is hurt. The bright but unacademic can, as we have seen, perform; but the performance is in-authentic and there is a pitiful loss of what they *could* be doing with intelligence, grace, and force. The average are anxious. The slow are humiliated. But also the authen-tically scholarly are ruined. Bribed and pampered, they forget the meaning of their gifts. As I have put it before, they "do" high school in order to "make" Harvard, and then they "do" Harvard.

I doubt that any of this rat-race is useful. Given quiet, and food and lodging, young scholars would study anyway, without grades. The drill and competitiveness are bad for their powers, and they mistake themselves and become snobbish craft-idiots. There is no evidence that highly creative youngsters in the sciences, arts, or professions, especially thrive on formal schooling at all, rather than by exploring and gradually gravitating to the right work and environment. For some, schooling no doubt saves time; for others it is interruptive and de-pressing. And on lower levels of performance, do the technical and clerical tasks of automated production really require so many years of boning and test-passing as is claimed? We have seen that the evidence is otherwise.

For urban poor kids who are cajoled not to drop out, the mis-education is a cruel hoax. They are told that the high school diploma is worth money, but we have seen that this is not necessarily so.

Of course, there is no real choice for any of them. Poor people must picket for better schools that will not suit most of their children and won't pay off. Farm youth must ride to central schools that are a waste of time for most of them, while they lose the remarkable competence they have. Middle-class youth must doggedly compete and be tested to death to get into colleges where most of them will doggedly (or cynically) serve time. It is ironical. With all the money spent on Research and Development, for hardware, computers, and tranquilizers, America can think up only one institution for its young human resources. Apparently the schooling that we have already had has brainwashed everybody.

## IX

This is the historical and social background out of which our young friend has come to that dazed look in the college classroom. He has been through a long process that has sapped his initiative, dampened his sexuality, and dulled his curiosity and probably even his intellect.

He is not earnest about what he is now doing. One would say that he is marking time, except that he does not have any particular ambition to step out.

What to do for him—or at least for the next generation of him?

Maybe the chief mistake we make is to pay too much *direct* attention to the "education" of children and adolescents, rather than providing them a worthwhile adult world in which to grow up. In a curious way, the exaggeration of schooling is both a harsh exploitation of the young, regimenting them for the social machine, and a compassionate coddling of them, since mostly they *are* productively useless and we want them to waste their hours "usefully."

## X

At the elementary level, especially in urban conditions, baby-sitting the children is indispensable. The schools both relieve the home and rescue the children from the home. But the criteria for baby-sitting are to be safe and enjoyable; our primary schools are safe enough but not enjoyable.

As a means of socialization and democratization, the primary schools have gone much too far toward regimentation. In my opinion, "good deportment" was always overstressed; but in the present conditions, when school is the only serious business of life and the classes are too crowded, it becomes spirit-breaking or a goad to defiance. And of course, in the new extraordinary pattern of suburbia and central city, the public schools are not even socially and racially mixed or equal in opportunity.

There is far too much bother about getting children to learn a set curriculum and to meet certain standards. Not that children are incapable of learning or do not want to learn; on the contrary, all the evidence is that even average children are capable and desirous of much more intellectual stimulation than they ever get in school, and with bright children this is astoundingly the case. Teachers and adults in general have a reponsibility to guess, provide means, offer the new, be available. But this is entirely different from assigning lessons and demanding performance, as if children did not have natural curiosity and wonder. Elementary schooling illustrates at its worst the human propensity to impose an unnecessary system and make it hard for ourselves, and thereby to lose the goods that are easy. Just nowadays, when we could be on the verge of a leisure culture, we would do well to consult the pedagogy of the Athenians, who were very cultivated citizens: they thought it was enough if the children played games, sang and acted Homer, and were taken around the city to see what went on. (Our word "school" is the Greek word for serious leisure.)

Most of these remarks are commonplaces of progressive education, and we should try that. (In fact progressive education has never been tried in this country, except in a few small schools for a few years.) Curiously, this seems to be the better judgment even of the National Science Foundation.


# XI


At the high school level, directly useful real activities would be more cultural than the average classroom for the average youth.

The liberal economists who propose using a larger share of production in the public sector are precisely not thinking of employing 15-year-olds; on the contrary, a chief motive of their plans is to diminish the unemployment of adults. But suppose, for a change, we think of the matter directly, without political overtones: on the one hand, there is a great amount of work that needs doing and has been shamefully neglected; on the other hand, there are millions of young people who could do a lot of it and are otherwise not well occupied. Further, it costs about $1000 a year to keep a youth in high school (and more than $2000 in a reform school); suppose we paid this money directly to the youth as he worked on an educative job.

Here are four great classes of youth jobs: construction—e.g. improving the scores of thousands of ugly small towns; community service and social work—like the Friends' Service, or working in understaffed hospitals or as school-aides, or janitoring public housing; assisting in the thousands of little theaters, independent broadcasters, and local newspapers, that we need to countervail the mass-media; and rural rehabilitation and conservation. For educational value for a majority of the young, I would match that curriculum against any four-year high school. By and large, too, these are not the areas proposed for big public works to create employment. Most likely nothing will be done about them at all.

Interestingly enough, the retraining and rehabilitation programs of the Departments of Labor and Justice contain better educational ideas, including schooling, than the direct school-aid bills. Since much of the Federal aid to education has been balked by the parochial school issue, some of the money has been better allotted *not* through the school systems!

Vocational training, including much laboratory scientific training, ought to be carried on as technical apprenticeships within the relevant industries. Certainly the big corporations have a direct responsibility for the future of their young, rather than simply skimming off the cream of those schooled, tested, and graded at the public expense.

Another indispensable part of the education of adolescents is the Youth House, the community of youth. This is miserably handled by the present neighborhood high schools, where there is a continual war of authority among school, home, and peer-group. James Coleman has forthrightly proposed that all high school students should be sent to schools on the other side of town, and if possible to be given room and board there. But again the present tendency is in just the opposite direction: to make the colleges community-colleges and commuting schools, so that the young will never get away on their own.

## XII

Thirdly, let me fit these ideas for secondary education into the framework of the colleges and universities.

The original purpose of the State universities and the land-grant colleges was to lead their communities, especially in the mechanical and agricultural arts. In this function, they would be admirable centers of administration and design of the public enterprises mentioned above: town improvement, broadcasting station, rural culture, health and community service. The value of any youth work camp depends on the worth of the project; the departments of the University could design the projects and give university-level guidance. Conversely, the students who come to the State universities would have been already working in the field on these projects, and the State universities could soft-pedal the present compulsory academic program that wastefully leads to 50% flunking.

By the same reasoning, the professional and graduate schools could work far more closely with the working professionals and industries in society, with whom their students would already have served apprenticeships as adolescents. This would avoid the present absurdity of teaching a curriculum abstracted from the work in the field, and then licensing the graduates to return to the field and relearn everything in terms of the actual work. And there would be less tendency for the contracted research that is appropriate to these institutes and professionals to dominate the curricula in all schools.

The liberal arts colleges, in turn, could resume their authentic intellectual tradition of natural philosophy, scholarship, and the humanities, without having to flirt with either narrowly technical research or hotel management. Academic high schools would, in effect, be prep schools for these colleges.

Finally, to fill a bad gap in our present framework of higher education, we need colleges for the altogether non-bookish, who nevertheless want to be informed and cultured citizens and to share in the experience of a college community. A model is to hand in the remarkable Danish Folk-Schools, where youngsters who have left school to go to work can return between the ages of 18 and 25, to learn oral history, current events, practical science and the politics of science, and to act plays and play music.

## XIII

These are a few speculations of one mind. My purpose is to get people at least to begin to think in another direction, to look for an organization of education less wasteful of human resources and social wealth than what we have. In reconstructing the present system, the right principles seem to me to be the following: To make it easier for youngsters to gravitate to what suits them, and to provide many points of quitting and return. To cut down the loss of student hours in parroting and forgetting, and the loss of teacher hours in talking to the deaf. To engage more directly in the work of society, and to have useful products to show instead of stacks of examination papers. To begin to decide what should be automated and what must not be automated, and to educate for a decent society in the foreseeable future.

To be candid, I do not think that we will change along these lines. Who is for it? The suburbs must think I am joking, I understand so little of status and salary. Negroes will say I am down-grading them. The big corporations like the system as it is, only more so. The labor unions don't want kids doing jobs. And the new major class of school-monks has entirely different ideas of social engineering.

Nevertheless, in my opinion, the present system is not viable; it is leading straight to 1984, which is not viable. The change, when it comes, will *not* be practical and orderly.

ACKNOWLEDGEMENTS

Acknowledgements are made to the publications in which some chapters of this book appeared in an earlier form: *The American Child* (National Committee on the Employment of Youth); *Harvard Educational Review; The School Dropout*, Daniel Schreiber, ed. (NEA Project: School Dropouts); *Channels* (Western Michigan University); *Commonweal; Orientation/1964*, a subsidiary of *motive* magazine (The Division of Higher Education of The Methodist Church, ©1964); *Playboy*.